T0347305

ROUTLEDGE LIBRARY EDITIONS:
RURAL HISTORY

Volume 4

POPULATION PERSISTENCE AND MIGRATION IN RURAL NEW YORK 1855-1860

POPULATION PERSISTENCE AND MIGRATION IN RURAL NEW YORK 1855-1860

DAVID PAUL DAVENPORT

Routledge
Taylor & Francis Group

LONDON AND NEW YORK

First published in 1989 by Garland Publishing, Inc.

This edition first published in 2018
by Routledge
2 Park Square, Milton Park, Abingdon, Oxon OX14 4RN

and by Routledge
711 Third Avenue, New York, NY 10017

Routledge is an imprint of the Taylor & Francis Group, an informa business

© 1989 David Paul Davenport

British Library Cataloguing in Publication Data
A catalogue record for this book is available from the British Library

ISBN: 978-1-138-89481-5 (Set)
ISBN: 978-1-315-11336-4 (Set) (ebk)
ISBN: 978-1-138-04573-6 (Volume 4) (hbk)
ISBN: 978-1-315-17165-4 (Volume 4) (ebk)

Publisher's Note
The publisher has gone to great lengths to ensure the quality of this reprint but points out that some imperfections in the original copies may be apparent.

Disclaimer
The publisher has made every effort to trace copyright holders and would welcome correspondence from those they have been unable to trace.

Population Persistence and Migration in Rural New York 1855-1860

David Paul Davenport

GARLAND PUBLISHING, INC.
New York   London
1989

Library of Congress Cataloging-in-Publication Data

Davenport, David Paul.
Population persistance and migration in rural New York, 1855–1860 /
David Paul Davenport.
p. cm. — (Garland studies in historical demography)
Includes bibliographical references.
ISBN 0-8240-3769-3 (alk. paper)
1. Rural-urban migration—New York (State)—History—19th century.
2, New York (State)—Population, Rural—History—19th century.
I. Title. II. Series.
HB1985.N5D38 1989
307.2'4'09747—dc20   89-23274

Printed on acid-free, 250-year-life paper

Manufactured in the United States of America

*To my parents Charles and Ruth Davenport
without whose support, both moral and financial,
I would have given up a long time ago*

ACKNOWLEDGEMENTS

I am indebted to a great number of people whose
cooperation and encouragement made this work possible.
Several deserve special recognition. Marnette Woolley of
the Champaign, Illinois, branch library of the
Genealogical Society of Utah cheerfully and promptly
handled my requests for materials from the main library in
Salt Lake City. Helene Farrell, her husband Jack, and her
able assistant, Mildred Motschmann, made my fieldwork at
the Old Stone Fort Museum/Library in Schoharie, New York,
enjoyable and rewarding. Carolyn White of the Social
Science Quantitative Laboratory at the University of
Illinois explained the mysteries of Probit and Multiple
Classification Analysis to me. Curtis Roseman and Vernon
Burton offered stimulating comments on earlier versions of
this manuscript. My grandmother, Lois Gray Davenport, and
my aunt, Ruth Davenport Johnson, fostered my interest in
the related fields of family history and genealogy. Mike
Broadway, Bob Kreger, David Cobb, Leslie Davis, and the
Rev. Ann Burger, encouraged my efforts and provided moral
support.

The University of Illinois provided essential
research support. Limited, but adequate, computer funds
aided data collection and analysis, and enabled production
of this typescript. The Graduate College awarded me a

dissertation research grant that made possible the acquisition of requisite microfilm. The Department of Geography subsidized my trip to Schoharie County with a grant from the summer field camp monies.

I also owe a debt of gratitude to the staffs of several libraries including the New York State Library at Albany, the New York Public Library, the American Geographical Society Library at the University of Wisconsin, Milwaukee, the Wisconsin State Historical Society Library at Madison, the Newberry Library, the Center for Research Libraries, and the Library of the University of Illinois. The assistance of the inter-library loan staff at the latter was particularly crucial, and they handled hundreds of requests from me with utmost efficiency.

Most of all I wish to say "Thanks" to my parents, Charles and Ruth Howell Davenport of Coalinga, California. Without their financial support, confidence in my abilities, and abiding love this work would not have been completed.

TABLE OF CONTENTS

LIST OF TABLES

LIST OF FIGURES

CHAPTER 1

INTRODUCTION

Migration was important in the demographic and areal growth of the United States during the nineteenth century. Immigrants swelled the country's cities and colonized its frontiers. Native-born Americans migrated from established farming areas and towns to nearby cities or nascent frontier communities and virgin lands in the West. Literature detailing the significance of migration in American urban growth and frontier settlement is both voluminous and well-known (Billington, 1960; Merk, 1978; Schlesinger, 1973; Wade, 1967; Ward, 1971; Weber, 1899). Some of these works have examined differential population persistence and social mobility within given cities and/or frontier areas (Curti, 1959; Knights, 1971; Thernstrom, 1964). Others, using diaries, census records, and documentary materials, have analyzed immigrant communities or described the westward movement (Jordan, 1966; Ostergren, 1981; Unruh, 1979; Yans-McLaughlin, 1977). None have studied population persistence and out-migration from long-settled rural areas of the United States. Thus, insights into the socio-demographic and economic characteristics which influenced different responses to the "migration offer" (Ellemers, 1964:52-53) by residents of a common place have not been gained.

This study examines population persistence and out-migration from a typical rural area of New York. The entire population of six representative towns(1) in Schoharie County as enumerated in the state census of 1855 constitutes the initial sample. For reasons detailed in Chapter 3, the population at risk analyzed statistically consists of 1,979 male heads of families. Three models of migration differentials are tested. The first explores the differences in socio-demographic and economic characteristics of migrants and non-migrants. The second investigates differentials between short-distance or partial displacement migrants and longer-distance or total displacement migrants. The third examines differentials between migrants to urban places and those to rural locales.

This research concludes that differences in the socio-demographic and economic characteristics of non-migrants and migrants are consistent with the differentials regularly observed in other studies of migration (Lee, 1966; Mangalam, 1968; Ravenstein, 1876, 1885, 1889; Shaw, 1975; Thomas, 1938). These indicate that life-cycle characteristics, place ties, economic condition, and other socio-demographic attributes of an individual are important migration differentials. The variables in this study that measure these attributes, include age, marital status, family size, and the number of children (life-cycle); prior migration experience, duration of residence, kinship, and landownership (place ties); occupation, economic rank, farm size and value, and the value of real and personal property (economic condition); and race and national origin (other socio-demographics).

Significant differentials among out-migrants are also found. The characteristics of partial displacement migrants differ from those of total displacement migrants in occupation, economic rank, and national origin. Occupation was the only significant differential between urbanward migrants and migrants to rural places.

Furthermore, previous research has implied that nearby cities and the frontier were foremost among the destinations of out-migrants from established farming districts. Both of these were important in terms of net population redistribution within the United States during the nineteenth century, but the conclusions of this study indicate that a majority of rural out-migrants moved to neither cities nor the frontier. Nearby rural areas were the most common destinations. The results of this research indicate that most out-migrants from rural areas of the northeastern United States during the nineteenth century moved relatively short-distances, a finding consistent with that of other researchers (Brown et al., 1970; Hagerstrand, 1947, 1962; Langholm, 1975; Miller, 1973; Ravenstein, 1876, 1885, 1889).

Development of an efficient, exhaustive procedure for tracing the sample population through time and space was an important aspect of this research. Using nominal records regularly used in studies of this type, I was able to identify 84 percent of the estimated survivors as either persisters or known migrants. Moreover, the percentage of those recovered using this methodology was even higher for male heads of families. The fate of a scant 8 percent could not be determined with complete assurance. Since the procedures included identifying those who died in situ, these eight percent were categorized as total displacement migrants. This study provides, then, the basis for a more comprehensive understanding of migration within the United States during the nineteenth century and a methodology for undertaking comparative works.

This study is organized as follows. Population change in American during the 1800s is examined in Chapter 2. Three inter-related topics are reviewed: frontier settlement, urbanization, and depopulation and emigration from rural areas of the northeastern United States. The sample population and the procedures used to trace these

people are discussed in Chapter 3. A model of
hypothesized differentials between migrants and
non-migrants is presented and tested in Chapter 4. The
destinations of out-migrants are examined and hypothesized
differentials between partial displacement migrants and
total displacement migrants and between urbanward migrants
and migrants to rural places are tested in Chapter 5. The
conclusions and significant findings of the research are
presented in Chapter 6.

Notes

1. A "town" in New York is a subdivision of a county
identical to townships in other parts of the United
States.

CHAPTER 2

MIGRATION IN NINETEENTH CENTURY AMERICA

Research dealing with migration and population change in the United States during the nineteenth century has focused on three themes: 1) settlement of the western frontier, 2) urban growth, and 3) European immigration. These studies invariably examine the origins of in-migrants resident at a given place and time. Rarely are out-migrants from a common origin of concern. Insights into population change from one time period to another have been gained however. It appears, for example, that only a minority of residents can be considered "persisters", people who appear in two successive population listings such as the manuscript census, tax records, and city directories (Curti, 1959; Katz, 1975; Thernstrom and Knights, 1971).

Three aspects of migration during the nineteenth century are addressed in this chapter. The first examines the westward movement and settlement of the frontier. Studies of population persistence are summarized, and the failure of historians to explicitly examine migration differentials noted. The second aspect discusses urbanization during the nineteenth century. Fertility and mortality differentials, immigration, and rural to urban migration within the United States are reviewed, as are findings concerning the persistence of urban dwellers. The third aspect focuses on depopulation and emigration from rural areas of New England and New York during the nineteenth century, processes occurring concomitantly with frontier settlement and urbanization. Together, these three aspects of migration during the nineteenth century provide a basic framework for this study of rural population persistence and out-migration.

The Frontier

Settlement of America's western frontier was a dynamic process involving people of varied cultural and economic backgrounds. Immigrants from Europe sought to begin their lives anew free of the rigid socio-economic structures in their native lands. American-born farmers, attracted by virgin, fertile soils of the interior, forsook the thin, overworked soils of the eastern seaboard. Non-farmers responded to the opportunities in business and manufacturing presented in the rapidly growing administrative, commercial, and industrial centers that served the rich agricultural districts of the West. Together these migrants to the frontier forged a uniquely American character representative of their common struggle against the "New World environment" (Turner, 1920).

Persistence on the Frontier

Historians of the frontier have not been explicitly concerned with migration differentials. Instead, they have focused attention on people already in the West. No one has attempted to ascertain whether or not the socio-demographic and economic characteristics of migrants differed significantly from those of non-migrants who remained at former common places of residence. Curti (1959), for example, called attention to the varied origins of the populace of Trempealeau County, Wisconsin, in the mid-1800s, but did not comment on how these recent in-migrants differed from their former neighbors who did not migrate.

Studies of population persistence are, though, suggestive of the characteristics that differentiate migrants from non-migrants. Curti (1959) found that those who persisted in Trempealeau from 1860 to 1870 were more likely than non-persisters to be older, married, born in the United States, and own real property valued at more than $1000. Moreover, farmers were more likely to remain than people with non-farm occupations. The proportion of persisters within each of these two occupational groups was also higher than among those individuals who called themselves farmers, but owned no land. Given all factors considered, Curti concluded that "differences in turnover are relatively small: the striking thing is the high percentage of turnover among all groups" (p. 69).

Findings by other scholars of frontier areas are remarkably similar to those of Curti (Table 2.1). In most frontier areas persisters were in the minority. Most farmers and non-farmers apparently responded positively to perceived opportunities elsewhere. Few people remained in one place long enough to participate in community development. Those who did were usually older, married, American-born, owners of real property.

However, a comparison of persisters and non-persisters is not the same as a comparison of non-migrants and migrants. In most respects persisters and non-migrants are comparable. Both terms refer to people who are found in situ at two successive dates. Non-persisters include not only out-migrants but persons who died and others who could not be traced due to omissions in the data or to methodological inadequacies. Thus, the characteristics of non-persisters are not synonymous with those of out-migrants from the area under study. Differentiation between non-migrants and out-migrants can only be made after subdividing the non-persisting population, a task that requires determining actual migration behavior of that population. Nevertheless, the differentials found important in studies of persistence are suggestive of those likely to be

TABLE 2.1

POPULATION PERSISTENCE IN THE WEST BY PERCENTAGE

Place	1850 1860	1860 1870	1870 1880	1880 1885	1880 1895
1. Blooming Grove, Wi.	75	56	60	--	--
2. Crawford Co., Ia.	--	20	27	--	--
3. Eastern Kansas	--	26	44.1	52.5	31.3
4. Grant Co., Wi.	--	--	--	44	21.5
5. Grass Valley, Ca.	4	--	--	--	--
6. Holland, Mich.	61	61	55	--	--
7. Mississippi (a)	28.3	--	--	--	--
8. Nevada City, Ca.	5	--	--	--	--
9. Nodaway Co., Mo.	32	--	--	--	--
10. Paris, Il.	38	--	--	--	--
11. Peel Co., Ontario (b)	48.9	--	--	--	--
12. Trempealeau Co., Wi.	--	25	29	--	--
13. Wapello Co., Ia.	30	--	--	--	--

a Farmers in Jefferson and Jones Counties
b 1851-1861

Sources: 1. Conzen, 1971:48.
            2. Bowers, 1960:23.
            3. Malin, 1935:365.
            4. Coleman, 1962:19.
            5. Mann, 1972:494.
            6. Kirk and Kirk, 1974:155.
            7. Weaver, 1945:28,113.
            8. Mann, 1974:494.
            9. Manring, 1978:407.
           10. Alcorn, 1974:691.
           11. Gagan and Mays, 1973:37.
           12. Curti, 1959:68.
           13. Thorne, 1959:310.

important migration differentials, regardless of the
community studied. Out-migrants from established farming
districts, particularly those in the North Atlantic
States, may be differentiated from non-migrants in the
same place by their age, marital status, and ownership of
real property --- this was certainly true of
non-persisters on the frontier --- but this question is
yet to be addressed. Thus conclusions about the effect of
socio-demographic and economic characteristics on
migration behavior are speculative, not definitive.

Urbanization

The nineteenth century witnessed dramatic growth
in the urban population of the United States (Table 2.2).
In 1800 less than four percent of the nation's populace
resided in cities of over 8,000 population. The six such
cities, Boston, Newport, New York City, Philadelphia,
Baltimore, and Charleston, were seaports largely dependent
upon trade with Europe for their existence. By
mid-century the number of cities with a population of at
least 8,000 had increased fourteen-fold and the percentage
of urban dwellers had tripled. The nation had expanded
westward to the Pacific Coast and cities had emerged in
the interior. Most were administrative or commercial
centers located where bulk breaking points ocurred on the

TABLE 2.2

URBAN GROWTH IN THE UNITED STATES, 1790-1900

Year	U.S. Population	Cities (a)		
		No.	Population	% of total
1790	3,929,214	6	131,472	3.35
1800	5,308,483	6	210,873	3.97
1810	7,239,881	11	356,920	4.93
1820	9,633,822	13	475,135	4.93
1830	12,866,020	26	864,509	6.72
1840	17,069,453	44	1,453,994	8.52
1850	23,191,876	85	2,897,586	12.49
1860	31,443,321	141	5,072,256	16.13
1870	38,558,371	226	8,071,875	20.93
1880	50,155,783	286	11,318,547	22.57
1890	62,622,250	448	18,284,385	29.20
--				
1890	62,947,714	---	17,913,894	28.50
1900	75,994,575	545	24,664,403	33.00

a the numerical definition of urban places was fixed
  at 8,000+ population by the Bureau of the Census for
  most of the nineteenth century (Truesdell, 1949).

sources: 1790-1890: Weber, 1899, p. 22.
         1890-1900: Weber, 1899, pp. 34-35.

nation's expanding transportation network but some, especially in the North Atlantic states, were major industrial centers.

Growth also was phenomenal in the second half of the century. By 1900 fully one-third of America's people resided in cities, a nearly three-fold increase in percentage over 1850. The number of cities also multiplied six and one-half times from 85 to 545. However, growth was not uniform nationally. The South was the most rural section of the country. More than half of the population in the West and North Atlantic regions were urban residents. In the latter fully 70 percent lived in cities, a fact closely associated with centralization of employment opportunities in manufacturing (Weber, 1904).

Causes of Urbanization

The disproportionate growth of America's cities during the nineteenth century may be attributed, in theory, to differential natural increase and/or net in-migration. The former would be the case, for example, if fertility rates were higher in urban than rural areas, and/or mortality rates higher in rural than urban areas, but evidence supports neither of these possibilities. Jaffee (1940:407-411) stated that urban birth rates were approximately 70 percent of those found in the countryside and that both declined at nearly equal rates from 1810 to 1840. Yasuba (1962) reached similar conclusions for the sixty year period beginning in 1800, but noted an upswing in urban fertility in the Northeastern States during the 1840s and 1850s that he attributed to the immigration and congregation of Irish and French-Canadian Catholics in cities of this region.

Bash (1963) conducted a study based upon fertility ratios, the number of children less than five years of age per 1,000 women aged 15-44, for 900 towns and cities in New York during the period from 1840 to 1875. In every instance the ratio in cities was less than that in the rest of the county in which the city was located. He also noted that by 1875 the rural-urban differential in fertility was nearly imperceptible because the fertility of the overwhelmingly urban foreign-born was as much as 13 percent higher than that of the native-born. Easterlin (1971:401) suggests that comparisons of rural and urban fertility must also take into account attitudes toward family limitation acquired at place of birth and upbringing. Consequently, if one eliminates the cases of foreign-born and native-born in-migrants, and examines only the fertility of women born in cities, the differential between rural and urban fertility again becomes pronounced.

Alternatively, natural increase in the urban population would have been greater than that of the rural population if mortality had been significantly higher among residents of rural areas. Evidence does not support this hypothesis however. Weber (1899:344) examined the Vital Statistics of New England for 1892 and concluded that: "The death-rate is the lowest in the rural parts and steadily increases with the size of the city." He examined this phenomenon further and observed that the greatest differences in rural and urban mortality occurred among children less than five years of age but that every cohort showed higher mortality among urban dwellers. Jaffee and Lourie (1942:352-371) also observed this relationship between mortality and city size in their study of the 1830 census returns. They found a difference of 19.8 deaths per thousand between the cities of Boston, New York, and Philadelphia and 46 rural New England towns. Vinovskis (1972:225-254) challenged their methodology but after adjusting their data for under-registration of rural deaths still concluded that urban mortality exceeded that of rural areas by 6.3 per thousand. Vinovskis also found that community size was most important when comparing mortality in places with less than 10,000 population with that in places with populations greater than 10,000. Among the former there was little difference in life expectancy by age cohort and sex but life expectancy was nearly ten years less for those under five years of age and about three years less for all other cohorts residing in places with populations greater than 10,000.

Condran and Crimmins (1980:179-202) examined mortality differentials between rural and urban areas in the northeastern United States in 1890 and 1900 and found that within individual states urban mortality was generally higher than rural mortality. They attributed the greater incidence of death in urban areas to several diseases associated with environmental contamination or close human contact. The greatest differential was observed in New York State where 2.29 deaths were reported in urban areas for each death reported in rural areas (p. 193). Condran and Crimmins also noted, as had Jaffee and Lourie (1942) and Vinovskis (1972), that the differential was greatest among infants and children less than five years of age (p. 194). This suggests that the studies of fertility differentials between rural and urban areas that have used child:women ratios as surrogates for birth registration statistics have under-estimated urban fertility. It remains clear, however, that urbanization of America's population in the nineteenth century did not result from higher rates of natural increase in cities than in rural areas of the country.

Migration and Urban Growth

The growth of American cities during the nineteenth century was a product of in-migration from Europe and rural America. Millions of people left their homes to begin anew in America's centers of commerce and industry. The Europeans came in two distinct waves. The first, from 1841 to 1860, was composed largely of immigrants from the British Isles and Germany. The second wave, which followed the Civil War, consisted of increasing proportions of Scadinavians, Eastern Europeans, and Southern Europeans. Although some miPrated from ports of entry to the rural frontier, most immigrants became urban residents. Bushee (1899:239) noted, for example, that:

> During the decade 1880-90 the total population of New York increased 26 percent, while her foreign element increased 34 percent; the population of Philadelphia in the same time increased 24 percent, and the foreign element 32 percent. The population of Boston during the decade 1885-1895 increased 27 percent, the foreign population 35 percent, and the element, found principally at the North End, composed of Italians and Russian Jews, increased 421 per cent.

However, Weber (1899:306) found that the concentration of foreigners in America's largest cities decreased in the period from 1850 to 1890. Although the foreign-born in the United States increased steadily from 9.68 percent in 1850 to 14.77 percent in 1890, the great cities, those with populations exceeding 100,000, acted as "centers of dispersion for immigrants" (p. 307). Most apparently went to cities of lesser size and not into the countryside for, as Weber notes, Willcox (1895) found that the percentage of foreign-born in the nation's fifty largest cities increased from 29.9 in 1880 to 30.8 in 1890.

Moreover, these figures mask the overwhelming significance of immigrants in the growth of American cities during the nineteenth century. Glasco (1973), for example, found that one-half of Buffalo's family heads in 1855 were German, one-fourth native-born Americans, and one-fifth Irish, a fact obscured in the published census by tabulation of birthplaces without regard to age and parentage. The native-born children of foreign born parents "inflated" the native-born component of the population. This is of considerable importance, given the higher fertility rates of immigrants. Immigrants and their native-born children were undoubtedly the dominant population group in many cities. Thus, much of the increase in the proportion of America's urban populace during the the nineteenth century can be attributed to the direct and indirect effects of immigration.

Rural to Urban Migration

Although of secondary importance, the cityward migration of rural Americans also was a factor in urban growth during the nineteenth century. Villages became cities as a result of in-migration from nearby rural areas and major centers of commerce and industry attracted in-migrants from nearby as well as more distant places. Bidwell (1917) found in his study of population growth in southern New England that expansion of maritime activities and the establishment of manufacturing enterprises in the period from 1810 to 1860 led to disproportionate urban growth. The twenty-six towns with populations exceeding 10,000 grew by 59 percent and the 371 towns with populations of 3,000 or less grew by only 2 percent. He attributed this to urbanward migration by rural residents of the region.

Tucker (1940:184) found that "the relative attraction of the city has been greater than that of the frontier in the United States since 1840 or earlier." More natives of Massachusetts and Rhode Island, for example, were in New York City in 1850 than in any one of fifteen frontier states (p. 173). Other authorities have reached similar conclusions. Shannon stated (1945:34) that:

> at least twenty farmers moved to town [between 1860 and 1900] for each industrial laborer who

moved to the land and ten sons of farmers went to the city for each one who became the owner of a new farm anywhere in the Nation.

Willcox (1895) attributed the decrease in interstate migration in the latter years of the nineteenth century to an increase in intra-state, rural to urban migration. Brown (1966:96) concluded that the cityward drift of population in Ohio replaced colonization on the western frontier as the dominant pattern during the 1880s. Sears (1960) found in his study of Philadelphia's growth from 1860 to 1910 that 42.5 percent of the city's population change was caused by in-migration of those born elsewhere in the United States. Moreover, a majority of these came from the nearby states of New York, Delaware, Maryland, and Virginia and from Pennsylvania's small towns and rural areas. Fletcher (1895a; 1895b) concluded that mechanization of agriculture had created a rural labor surplus that could only find work in cities. This cityward drift of population was in Fletcher's opinion "unmistakeably from the farms to the nearest village, from the village . . . to the city" (1895b:737).

Evidence of rural to urban migration was also found by Jensen, Stephenson, and Webster (1978) in their study of residential persistence within New York from 1875 to 1880.(1) The percentage of people living on farms or in towns with fewer than 2,500 residents declined from 30.5 in 1875 to 22.5 in 1880 (p. 100). Slightly more than

8 per cent of all migrants moved to New York City, but the greatest shift was into small urban places. In 1875 15.2 percent of the sample population resided in towns of 2,500 to 10,000 people. In 1880 this figure was 46.3 percent.

Weber (1899) concluded in his study of urban growth in Europe and the United States during the nineteenth century that rural to urban migration was important in both world regions. Among his examples was that of Boston in 1885, where the state census indicated that 11 percent of the city's residents had been born elsewhere in Massachusetts (p. 265). He concluded (p. 288) that:

> It is not true, as Mr. Ravenstein [1889], for example, seems inclined to think, that "the migratory current from the country to the city is scarcely perceptible in the United States and other newly settled countries."

Rural to urban migration was an important factor in growth of American cities during the nineteenth century.

Urban Population Persistence

Urban growth was not a steady, additive process. Although the population of any given city might register an increase from one year to another, cities were not, to borrow an analogy from Thernstrom and Knights (1971:19), piles of bricks added to by in-migration but never subtracted from by out-migration. Urban populations were, instead, extremely fluid. Population change in Boston, a city of 363,000 in 1880, is perhaps representative. Thernstrom and Knights (1971) estimated the annual in and out migration for the city and concluded that although the total population increased by 67,179 during the 1880s, nearly 800,000 people had actually taken up residence in the city at some time during the decade. Only 64 percent of the adult males resident there in 1880 remained throughout the decade (p. 24).

Moreover, persistence in Boston during the 1880s was actually quite high in comparison with other cities and decades (Table 2.3). Research generally indicates that only a minority of any given city's residents could be found in the same city after ten years. Younger cities, particularly those in the West, seem to have had lower rates of persistence than longer settled places, but the population of all urban places, large and small, East and West, was highly mobile.

Other scholars argue that the high mobility implied by low persistence rates is illusory. Allen (1977) indicates, for example, that persistence of the total population was undoubtedly higher than that reported for male-only samples. Since males were more likely to migrate than females, overall persistence rates must be adjusted upwards an average of 15 percent (p. 581). Moreover, differences between cities in different regions

TABLE 2.3

POPULATION PERSISTENCE IN SELECTED CITIES BY PERCENTAGE

Place	1830 1840	1840 1850	1850 1860	1860 1870	1870 1880	1880 1890
Boston, Massachusetts	44	39	39	--	--	64
Denver, Colorado	--	--	--	--	37	27
Hamilton, Canada	--	--	35	--	--	--
Houston, Texas	--	--	33	--	--	--
Indianapolis, Indiana	--	--	--	--	69	71
Jacksonville, Illinois	--	--	28	24	--	--
Los Angeles, California	--	--	--	--	--	54
Omaha, Nebraska	--	--	--	--	--	44
Philadelphia, Pa.	30	38	32	--	--	--
Poughkeepsie, New York	--	--	--	49	50	--
St. Louis, Missouri	--	--	15	--	--	36
Salem, Massachusetts	--	--	38	--	--	--
San Antonio, Texas	--	--	--	--	32	--
San Francisco, Ca.	--	--	24	--	48	50
South Bend, Indiana	--	--	18	16	26	--
Waltham, Massachusetts	54	56	44	45	50	58
Worcester, Ma.	--	--	34	--	--	--

Sources: Boston (Thernstorm, 1973:222-223)
          Denver (Tank, 1978:211)
          Hamilton (Katz, 1975:123, Table 3.3)
          Houston (Jackson, 1978:268, Table 3)
          Indianapolis (Barrows, 1981:200)
          Jacksonville (Doyle, 1978:96n)
          Los Angeles (Thernstrom, 1973:222-223)
          Omaha (Thernstrom, 1973:222-223)
          Philadelphia (Thernstrom, 1973:222-223)
          Poughkeepsie (Thernstrom, 1973:222-223)
          St. Louis (Hodes, 1973:151-156, Tables 95, 96)
          Salem (Doherty, 1977:31)
          San Antonio (Thernstrom, 1973: 222-223)
          San Francisco (Thernstrom, 1973:222-223)
          South Bend (Esslinger, 1975:43, Table 3-4)
          Waltham (Thernstrom, 1973:222-223)
          Worcester (Doherty, 1977:31)

disappear when the age and sex structure of these places is taken into account.

Jensen et al. (1978) raise other criticisms. They believe that the migratory propensity of urban populations is greatly exaggerated because of errors in nominal tracing. Three problems co-exist. First, mortality sometimes is not taken into account. Only in recent studies have researchers recognized that the sample population must be decomposed and the number of survivors estimated before computing persistence rates. Second, "hiders", persons who because of their behavior or the oversights of those compiling nominal records, won't be found. For example, city directories were more haphazard in listing recent in-migrants and lower-class people than others (Goldstein, 1954; Knights, 1969). Census manuscripts, ostensibly enumerations of the entire population, are known to have overlooked the urban poor who often resided in "dangerous" and uninviting neighborhoods and rural folk who lived in remote, inaccessible areas. An estimated 7 to 10 percent undercount resulted. Other people, particularly immigrants, may have changed their surnames in an effort to be assimilated more rapidly. Curti (1959:67), for example, cited the case of the Swedish Lewis (nee Larson) family. Jensen et al. (1978) estimate that 20 percent of any given sample population are "hiders" (p. 88f). Third, "errors" are common. They note (p. 88c) that:

> Comparison of copies of Pennsylvania manuscript census returns for 1800 made independently by two highly qualified genealogists reveals [surname] discrepancies on the order of 10 percent.

Names often are misspelled from one census year to the next and prefixes in surnames occasionally are dropped. The result of these kinds of nominal inconsistencies is that 10 to 20 percent of any sample population will not be traceable (p. 88). When all three sources of tracing error are considered, Jensen et al. (1978:88g) believe that the amount of geographic mobility estimated by historians of the nineteenth century has been:

> greatly exaggerated. Turnover was high --- but not nearly as high as purported when it is casually assumed that everyone who is not traced in the same place must have migrated.

Importantly, the socio-demographic and economic factors associated with persistence in the cities are consistent with those on the frontier. Persisters are always older, probably native-born, and more likely to own real property than non-persisters. Criticism about the method of computing persistence rates and the failure of most to decompose the non-persisting members of the sample population not withstanding, it remains clear that there are important differences between non-migrants and migrants, be they residents of frontier communities or cities.

Population Change in Rural America

Emigration and depopulation have been called "neglected aspects of population geography" (Lowenthal and Comitas, 1962). Few scholars have focused on either of these often related phenomena, yet, both are important elements of the American demographic experience. This was particularly true during the nineteenth century. Although the population of the United States as a whole grew rapidly and steadily throughout the century, not every town and county did so. Population growth was closely associated with urban development and colonization of the western frontier. Concomitant depopulation occurred in older settled areas that experienced reduced in-migration and eventually net out-migration.(2)

Zelinsky (1962) is alone in having examined this phenomenon in the United States on a national scale. His exploratory and largely descriptive study of rural population change mapped the peak years of population by county and developed a typology of demographic change. Depopoulation occurred first in the New England states where it was well advanced by 1840 (Fig. 2.1). By 1860 it had enveloped most of New England and adjacent New York. At the close of the nineteenth century rural depopulation was widespread in the North Atlantic region.

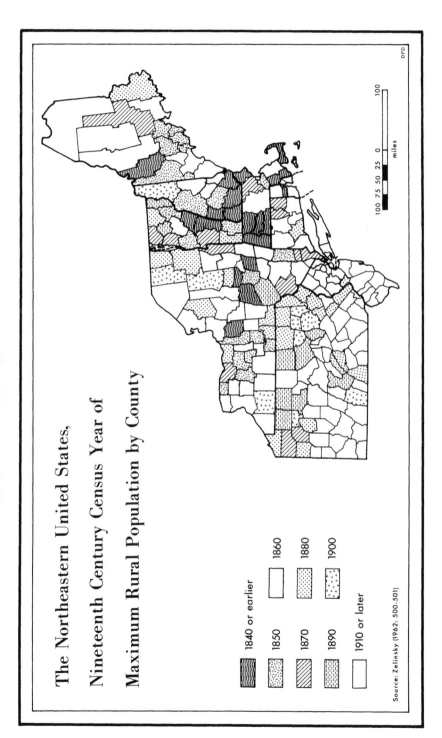

The Northeastern United States,

Nineteenth Century Census Year of

Maximum Rural Population by County

1840 or earlier

1850

1860

1870

1880

1890

1900

1910 or later

Source: Zelinsky (1962: 500-501)

100 75 50 25 0   100

miles

DPD

Figure 2.1

Fletcher (1895a, 1895b) demonstrated that this was true at the town level in several mid-western and northeastern states. Although the total populations of Ohio, Indiana, Illinois, Iowa, Michigan, and New York increased between 1880 and 1890, more than half, and in the case of New York more than two-thirds, of the towns or townships suffered population losses. He attributed this to the effects of agricultural mechanization.

Wilson's insightful study in 1936 of population change in northern New England suggests though depopulation was related to more than simple farm abandonment. The rural decline was a general one involving farmer, merchant, and artisan alike. Diminishing returns in agriculture invariably led to a decline in business in rural villages. As farmers left, demand for the services rendered by shoemakers, tailors, etc. became negligible. Throughout many parts of New England the scene must have been similar to that described by Charles C. Nott in The Nation of November 21, 1889.

> Midway between Williamstown and Brattleboro, I saw on the summit of a hill against the evening sky what seemed a large cathedral. Driving thither, I found a huge, old-time, two-story church, a large academy (which blended in the distance with the church), a village with a broad street, perhaps 150 feet wide. I drove on and found that the church was abandoned, the academy dismantled, the village deserted. The farmer who owned the farm on the north of the village lived on one side of the broad street and he who owned the farm on the south lived on the other, they were the only inhabitants. All of the others had gone --- to

the manufacturing villages, to the great cities, to the West. Here had been industry, education, religion, comfort, and contentment, but there remaine only a dreary solitude of forsaken homes. . . . The deserted village was the old-fashioned "Centre" of the town, on a high hill, remote from the railways and millstreams, unknown to summer boarders --- an agricultural village, dependent upon the agriculture around it and from which it sprang.

Conditions were no better in rural New York. M. A. Veder of Lyons reported in The Nation of November 28, 1889 that:

In the rural districts of Wayne County [contiguous to Monroe County that contains Rochester] there are no less than 400 empty houses. It is a lamentable fact that the rural population of Wayne County is slowly drifting into the larger towns and cities, while many are going West in search of cheaper homes or fortunes. The town of Sodus alone has over fifty deserted houses, and Huron has thirty or more. The next census will show a marked decrease in the rural population as compared with ten years ago.

Although many contemporaries were negative in their assessment of the effects of rural depopulation, Barron (1980) found that life in Chelsea, Vermont, a town that declined in population from 1840 to 1900 by nearly one-half, "was characterized by increasing economic, demographic, and social stability" (p. 185). Moreover, the town economy suffered little, if any, during the period. The number of farms, their size, and their production remained relatively constant. Most farmers raised sheep at mid-century and continued to do so. The reduced supply of labor occasioned by lessened in-migration, and out-migration highly selective of farm laborers and young men, forced a reduction in the size of flocks, but farmers responded by upgrading the quality of their sheep. The resultant increase in the quantity of wool per animal prevented a decline in agricultural and hence business fortunes.

Might this also have been the case in other parts of New England? Improved crop yields, for example, might have meant sowing less acreage at no loss in profit. If this were the case --- and research supporting this viewpoint is yet to appear --- then the land abandonment so widely reported in The Nation and other periodical literature of the day was not necessarily bad for the local economy. Instead it represented a rational adjustment to the emigration of labor.

Out-Migration by Rural Americans

Regardless of the implications of rural depopulation during the nineteenth century, its causes can be readily identified. Declining fertility and decreased in-migration cannot be dismissed entirely, but neither was as important as emigration. Tens of thousands of people departed for better opportunities elsewhere. The frontier was one such place, especially for Yankees. Wilson states (1936:56-57) that:

> The Midwest, and later the trans-Missouri
> territory, acted . . . as a magnet which
> attracted the ambitious youth of the hill country
> as well as its discontented farmers.

By 1850 more than two million people of New England origin

resided outside the region (Turner, 1935:44).

New Yorkers also contributed significantly to the

populace of the West. The Schoharie Patriot (July 15,

1855), commenting on the state census returns of 1855,

noted that:

> From the returns thus far published, it would seem
> that the rate of increase of population in the
> State during the last five years has not been as
> great as formerly. There has been a large gain in
> most of the cities; the villages, also, have
> generally increased somewhat but the rural
> districts show little, if any, increase, owing, it
> is presumed, to a continual westward emigration.

The cityward drift of New England's rural

population was also evident. Factory towns in the

Merrimack and Blackstone River Valleys drew upon rural

areas of New England for their labor early in the century.

Farm girls were especially sought for they proved to be

adept at mastering the skills required in textile mills.

In 1845 the majority of hands in the factories of Lowell,

Massachusetts, were girls from rural New England (Miles,

1845). Moreover, the occupational structure of all New

England was being altered by the establishment of

water-powered mills at what seems to have been every site

in the region with potential. By 1850, only half of the

region's gainfully employed males were engaged in farming

(Wilson, 1936:68-72). Some of these mills did not survive infancy but others formed the cores of nascent cities. Employees of those firms that did not survive undoubtedly secured employment with those that did, rather than return to agricultural pursuits. Thus, the tendency of the population at mid-century was toward agglomeration.

Migration Selectivity

Although the literature suggests that migration was selective of young adults, males, and those with better education, it has not been established firmly that migrants were different than non-migrants at a common residential origin. Two basic questions need to be addressed. Were emigrants "average" residents of the rural areas in which they originated or did they possess different socio-demographic and economic characteristics from their non-migrating neighbors? Which of these characteristics seem to be most closely associated with distance migrated and the type of destination selected?

Neither of these questions has been adequately addressed in studies of migration during the nineteenth century, but a "profile" of typical emigrants from Vermont is offered by Stillwell (1937). His study was based on the biographies of nearly 8,000 Vermont-born men found in hundreds of county histories published during the latter years of the nineteenth century. He concluded that the bulk of Vermont's emigrants in the period from 1790 to 1860 were farmers looking for better lands and that the professions of education, law, and medicine were also disproportionately represented. So, too, were skilled craftsmen. Moreover, most of the emigrants were young. Three-quarters were under the age of thirty when they left Vermont; half were under the age of twenty-five.

Stillwell (1937) also noted that Vermonters were consistently clannish. Although their destinations were widely distributed throughout the mid-western and Middle Atlantic states, "specific towns in the west were populated from specific towns in Vermont. Old neighbors were new neighbors" (p. 241).

Vermonters were not unique in this respect. Migration to any specific locale is often "channelized," or or directed to that place from specific places of origin (MacDonald and MacDonald, 1964; Roseman, 1971a). This was especially true of immigrants from Europe during the nineteenth century (Akerman, Kronborg, and Nilsson, 1977; Kirk and Kirk, 1974; Ostergren, 1976). A particular destination was chosen because friends, relatives, and former neighbors had established homes there. The correspondence of these earlier migrants provided potential migrants with encouragement and information needed to evaluate the likely destination and the journey to the New World was occassionally facilitated with pre-paid tickets (Erickson, 1972; Ritchey, 1976; Svalestuen, 1977). Migration to specific places in North America became a tradition in some European communities (Kero, 1977).

Channelization was also important in the migration of native-born Americans to the frontier. Movement was generally East to West within relatively narrow bands of latitude (Conzen, 1974; Meyer, 1976; Zelinsky, 1973). This was especially true of farmers who had acquired skills associated with particular soil types and climates. New Englanders and New Yorkers, for example, settled predominantly in northern Ohio, Michigan, and other areas of the upper mid-west (Holbrook, 1950; Mathews, 1909). Frontiersmen in southern Indiana and Illinois and southeastern Iowa came largely from Kentucky, Tennessee, and Virginia (Bogue, 1963). Northeastern Texas was peopled from Tennessee, southern Missouri, and Arkansas (Lathrop, 1948). Except in major urban centers, and usually only among those engaged in the medical or legal professions, banking, manufacturing, or commerce, there were few Northerners in the South and vice versa.

Many communities on the frontier were created by settlers with common origins. Although American-born pioneers on the Dakota frontier had come from places "widely scattered behind the frontier" channelization is evident in larger-scale analysis (Hudson, 1976:103). Contiguous tracts of land in Sanborn County, South Dakota, were homesteaded, for example, by families from Oneida County, New York, from the area around Aurora and Joliet, Illinois, and from various Norwegian colonies in Wisconsin, Illinois, Minnesota, and Michigan, respectively (Hudson, 1973). Likewise, Bowen (1978) analyzed the origins of Oregon's populace in 1850 and found that settlements in the Willamette Valley were dominated by kinship groups and neighbors from the same communities in the East.

Stillwell (1937) also reached a conclusion about gender differences in migration selectivity. The 1850 census revealed a deficit of 6,000 females in Vermont, "extraordinary given the large number of known male emigrants" (p. 211). He concluded that "it seems perfectly clear that the [Vermont] girls were going, independently, and in large numbers, to the cities of the East" (p. 211). Thus, it appears that emigration from Vermont, at least through 1850, was gender selective by destination, a conclusion that supports Ravenstein's "laws of migration" (1885; 1889).

Stillwell's work is seminal in the study of out-migration, but it is deficient in two respects. First, his sample is biased. It is well-known that people included in the published county histories paid for this privilege. Most were undoubtedly among the wealthiest members of their respective communities. Thus, the sample does not include Vermonters who remained members of the working class. This could influence conclusions about the distance migrated, the character of destinations, the youth of emigrants --- in fact, about all of the characteristics of a typical emigrant. Second, Stillwell did not compare his sample population with a group of non-migrants. Thus, while it may be true that emigrants from Vermont were young, he did not demonstrate that they were younger than non-migrants. The observed age distribution may simply be a reflection of Vermont's demographic structure during the time period examined. Without these comparisons the questions of selectivity remain unanswered.

Summary

The traditional view of migration within the United States during the nineteeth century implies that emigrants from rural areas experiencing depopulation went to either the frontier or into nearby cities. This appears to have been the case for rural out-migrants in New England and, presumably, the North Atlantic states in general. However, this view is not founded on empirical studies. Scholars have noted the origin of settlers on the frontier and of residents in important cities, but no one has examined the entire population of a community in the rural Northeast and analyzed the response of each potential migrant to the migration offer. Thus, conclusions about migration selectivity during the nineteenth century and the destinations of emigrants must be considered tentative. The following research addresses these issues. First, it analyzes the characteristics of those who migrated and those who didn´t. Second, it investigates the out-migration field and the socio-demographic and economic correlates associated with the destinations of out-migrations. Thus, it provides insights into an unexplored topic in the historical geography and demography of the nineteenth century.

Notes

1. This unpublished work is available from the Family and Community History Center of the Newberry Library, 60 West Walton Street, Chicago, Illinois 61801. An abridged version titled "Migration and Mobility in Late Nineteenth and Early Twentieth Century America" was sumbitted by Stephenson as his Ph. D. thesis in history (University of Wisconsin-Madison, 1980), but it is not available from University Microfilms International.

2. My comments concerning rural depopulation and emigration during the nineteenth century have been confined largely to the New England states. This was not by design. I had planned to include material illustrative of these processes within New York State, but little exists. The rural populace of New York was subjected to the same causative factors as the residents of New England but Yorkers left fewer published records which might have

provided substance for this study. Moreover, secondary sources like those of Stillwell (1937) and Wilson (1936) have yet to appear for New York. I expected Ehrlich's (1972) "Development of Manufacturing in Selected Counties in the Erie Canal, Corridor, 1815-1860" to provide statistics of employee nativity but it did not. However, in the chapter that follows it will be demonstrated that the study area in New York is representative of the northeastern states as a whole thus making the foregoing discussion of emigration from rural New England relevant to this work.

CHAPTER 3

METHODS AND MATERIALS OF STUDY

Studies of nineteenth century migration in the United States have been hampered by a lack of adequate data. Unlike some European countries, the United States has never maintained population registers that record every change of residence by an individual during his or her lifetime within the respective country (Thomas, 1938, Appendix C). Instead, students of American migration must use data sources that are in themselves useful only for studies of in-migration. These usually record birthplaces by country and state or territory within the United States, but give no indication as to the destinations of those who emigrate.

Several scholars have studied migration by examining population persistence. They have linked nominal data sources and compared the characteristics of persisters, those found in sequential population listings, with non-persisters, those not found. Persisters are regarded as non-migrants but non-persisters include three groups of people with potentially different characteristics. These three are: 1) those who emigrated, 2) those who died in situ and were not at risk to either emigrate or persist throughout the entire period under study, and 3) those who persisted but were not found because of errors in data sources and/or research methodology. The conclusions of these studies regarding migration differentials should be considered tentative, not definitive.

Complete decomposition of a sample population is rarely attempted. Persisters are readily recovered using nominal record linkage, but differentiating among non-persisters is a difficult task. Knights (1971) and Jensen, Stephenson, and Webster (1978) had limited success in tracing emigrants, and pessimistic statements by Thernstrom (1968:167) that:

> There is no feasible method of tracing individuals once they disappear from the community under consideration

and by Chudacoff (1972:70) that "Almost all who emigrate left for parts unknown" certainly discourage further efforts to do so.

Application of a model life table has been offered as one method of dealing with the effects of mortality. Katz (1975) and Barron (1980) estimated the number of survivors, and found that previous research has underestimated persistence rates. Although conceptually sound, this method fails to differentiate those who died in situ from those who died after migrating. Instead it assumes that those who died all did so in situ. The importance of this difference lies in defining the population at risk. Those who die in situ must be subtracted from the population at risk to either persist or emigrate because they did not survive throughout the period under study. Those who migrated and then died exhibited the behavior being evaluated and must, therefore, be retained in the sample population. Model life tables cannot tell the researcher who d`ed in situ and who after migrating. Estimates of mortality are poor substitutes for actual mortality figures derived from vital records, obituaries, and headstone inscriptions.

The third group of non-persisters, those who persist but are not identified as such, is potentially the most problematic. Jensen, Stephenson, and Webster (1978:88e) called these individuals "hiders" and estimated that twenty percent of their total population fell into this category. Underenumeration in census manuscripts and other population listings such as directories is well-known. The researcher can do little to overcome errors in original handwritten records but should make every effort to correctly interpret and transcribe nominal records. The greatest difficulty exists with inconsistently spelled names. Census enumerators and directory canvasers often dropped surname prefixes (e.g. de la, Van, O´) and also adopted phonetic spellings for what were to them unfamiliar family names. For example, Marshall became Martial, Teneyck became De Nike, and Auchampaugh became Okampaw. Recovering foreign born people who Americanize their names is a seemingly impossible task that can be accomplished by examining all available information pertaining to the family group and not just the individual in question. For example, one would not know that Lutewis Schworm was, five years later, Ludwig Swan, unless one compared the ages of both men, knew both to be born in Baden, Germany, and knew that both had German-born wives named Caroline. A thorough, exhaustive perusal of all possible nominal records is the only assurance that the number of unfound persisters has been minimized.

In this study I devised a system of tracing a sample population of nearly 12,000 men, women, and children, aged 0 through 99, that identified 79 percent of them as either persisters or out-migrants. This percentage increased to 84 after estimates of mortality were made. Moreover, I was able to fully decompose the 2,089 male heads of families in the sample. Perusal of census manuscripts and city directories recovered 87 percent of these, and obituaries, headstone inscriptions, and comparisons of census family composition established the actual mortality of 61 percent of the estimated deaths. The whereabouts of a scant 7.5 percent of the male heads of families could not be determined, but given the thorough search procedures utilized I categorized these people as long-distance migrants.

This chapter is concerned with four aspects of the methods and materials utilized in this study of population persistence and migration in rural New York. First, selection of the sample population is discussed. Second, the procedures for decomposition of this sample are detailed. Third, the biases in recovery of this sample are presented. Fourth, decomposition of male heads of families, the principle migration decision makers in the sample population, is addressed.

The Sample

Population sampling is a technique commonly used by social scientists and adopted by some historians during the past decade. In practice this has meant that individuals or households have been selected at random or in a systematic stratified manner from a nominal data source. Two works are illustrative of this practice. Jensen, Stephenson, and Webster (1978) drew a sample of about 2,000 families from the 1875 New York State Census by randomly selecting families from existing manuscript schedules first "stratified and clustered in order to approximate the residential distribution of the state" (p. 83). Morgan and Golden's study (1979) of Holyoke, Massachusetts was based upon every tenth, non-institutional household in the 1880 census.

Selection of individuals for study using either of these methods was deemed inappropriate for two reasons. First, the methodology developed for tracing emigrants was based in part upon birthplace and required that the entire sample be drawn from the same county. Second, measurement of kinship ties was based upon frequencies of surnames in the town of enumeration. Skipping families would render this tabulation impossible. Thus, for methodological and analytical purposes my initial sample consisted of whole populations of representative towns.

The Study Area

Schoharie County, centered forty miles southwest of Albany, was a typical rural area of New York in the 1850s (Fig. 3.1). The majority of its workforce was engaged in farming but sizable minorities were laborers, craftsmen, businessmen and civil servants, or in the learned professions (Table 3.1). Schoharie's farmers had faced the same adversities of western competition, seasonal labor shortages, and soil exhaustion, and made the same adjustments as farmers elsewhere in the state (Anderson, 1925; Leaman and Conkling, 1975). At the beginning of the nineteenth century the county was renowned for for its prodigious wheat crops, but in the 1850s butter and cheese were the principle cash crops.

Figure 3.1

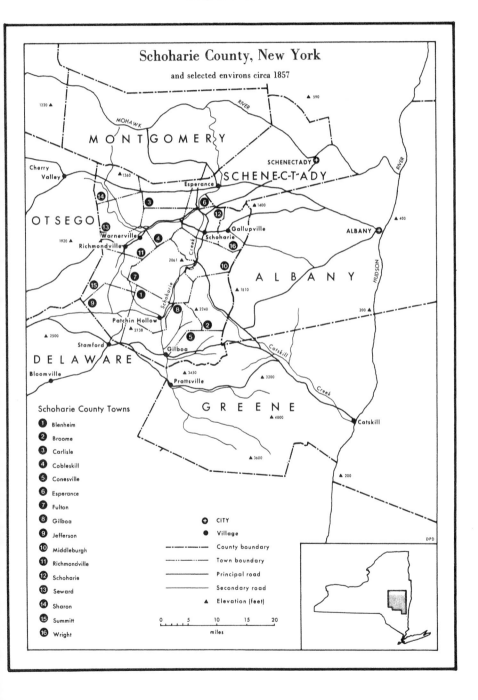

Schoharie County, New York

and selected environs circa 1857

Schoharie County Towns

1. Blenheim
2. Broome
3. Carlisle
4. Cobleskill
5. Conesville
6. Esperance
7. Fulton
8. Gilboa
9. Jefferson
10. Middleburgh
11. Richmondville
12. Schoharie
13. Seward
14. Sharon
15. Summitt
16. Wright

CITY

Village

County boundary

Town boundary

Principal road

Secondary road

Elevation (feet)

0 5 10 15 20
miles

TABLE 3.1

OCCUPATIONS OF
SCHOHARIE COUNTY RESIDENTS IN 1855 (1)
(percentages)

Businessmen	375	(4.00)
Civil Servants	171	(1.83)
Craftsmen	1506	(16.08)
Farmers	5372	(57.36)
Laborers	1613	(17.22)
Learned Professions	158	(1.69)
Service Workers	125	(1.33)
Uncategorized	46	(0.49)

	9366	
	----	

1 A complete listing compiled from Hough,
  1857:178-195 is found in Appendix A.

Like other New York farmers, those in Schoharie were diversified. Most raised coarse grains for animal feeds and distilling, fruits and vegetables for home consumption and seasonal marketing, and a specialty cash crop as a buttress against the vagaries of the dairy trade. In Schoharie the latter included hops, buckwheat, and clover seed.

Several statistical comparisons also suggest that Schoharie County was representative of rural New York in 1855 (Table 3.2). Of these only the percentage of alien residents might be considered atypical. This percentage was more than one standard deviation less than the average for all rural towns in the state, a fact I attribute to the lack of "modern" transportation within Schoharie. Neither canal nor rail passed through the county in 1855 and, given Schoharie's economic structure, few immigrants would have had reason to purposely seek employment and reside there in 1855. Moreover, most aliens were recently arrived common laborers who were no longer in the county in 1860.

Schoharie's demographic patterns were also remarkably similar to those of New York as a whole (Fig. 3.2). Its age and sex structure was comparable to that of the entire state and its death rates were not significantly different from those of the entire state. Moreover, depopulation, a phenomenon that first affected

TABLE 3.2

STATISTICAL COMPARISONS OF SCHOHARIE COUNTY AND RURAL NEW YORK STATE

CHARACTERISTIC	NEW YORK (1)	SCHOHARIE	(Z-SCORE)
Percentage black and mulatto	0.64	1.36	(.9069)
Percentage alien	8.05	2.61	(-1.23)
Average family size	5.30	5.36	(.0822)
Percentage landowners	14.59	13.65	(-.4772)
Percentage illiterate (2)	2.47	3.07	(.4082)
Mean dwelling value	$433.97	$451.87	(.1129)
Percentage improved acreage (3)	55.00	63.32	(-.4271)
Mean value per acre of farmland	$ 29.87	$ 27.93	(-.1160)
Mean farm size (4)	112.06	127.59	(.8925)

1. N of 744 excludes all towns in New York, Richmond, Kings, and
   Queens counties, all incorporated areas, and all towns containing
   village with populations upwards of 1000 (see Hough, 1857:18-23).
2. Reported in the census for persons age 20 or more years of age.
   Computations not adjusted for undetermined inter-town differences
   in age structure.
3. Percentage of total farmland which I assume to be something less
   than total town acreage. Actual size of each town in 1855 could
   not be ascertained.
4. The number of farms was reported by county in 1850 but not in 1855.
   Average farm size was computed using the total farm acreage
   reported in 1855 and the number of farms reported in 1850.

Sources: Debow (1854) and Hough (1857)

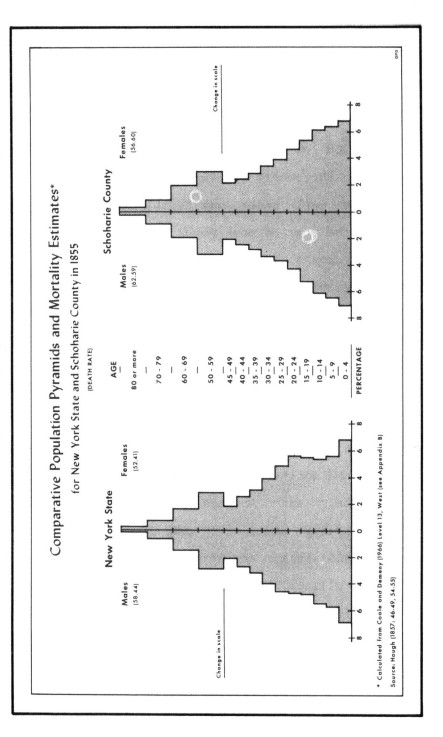

Figure 3.2

rural areas of New England in the 1790s, had reached
Schoharie and three adjoining counties by mid-century. In
1855, the sixteen towns comprising Schoharie County had a
combined population of 33,519, twenty-nine fewer than
enumerated in 1850 (Table 3.3). A resurgence associated
with construction of the Albany and Susquehanna Railroad
was recorded for the county as a whole in 1860, but farm
abandonment was well under way by this date. For most
towns 1850 was the year of peak population.

The six towns of Blenheim, Esperance, Gilboa,
Richmondville, Schoharie, and Wright, whose residents in
1855 comprise the sample population, were representative
of Schoharie County in that year. Three increased in
population between 1850 and 1855. Three did not. Two
contain thin soils associated with the rugged uplands of
the Catskill Mountains. Four contain more fertile soils
associated with the valleys of Schoharie Creek and its
tributaries in the northern section of the county. In one
town, Schoharie, was located the county's largest
settlement and county seat, the courthouse village of
Schoharie with 855 souls. Another town, Gilboa, contained
a textile mill village of nearly 450 people and two
crossroads hamlets of 25-40 persons each. A third town,
Richmondville, contained the villages of Richmondville and
Warnerville, settlements with populations of 180-200. The
Town of Esperance, in the county's northeast, was bisected

TABLE 3.3

POPULATION CHANGE IN SCHOHARIE COUNTY, 1850-1865

Town	1850	Pct. Change	1855	Pct. Change	1860	Pct. Change	1865
Blenheim	1314	3	1351	1	1367	-12	1199
Broome	2268	-6	2138	2	2182	-10	1969
Carlisle	1817	-5	1723	2	1760	0	1700
Cobleskill	2229	-1	2208	7	2357	3	2439
Conesville	1582	-11	1407	5	1478	-8	1359
Esperance	1428	-4	1370	3	1409	-2	1383
Fulton	2566	9	2817	4	2944	-5	2808
Gilboa	3024	-12	2657	-4	2541	-6	2385
Jefferson	1748	-3	1688	2	1716	0	1718
Middleburgh	2967	3	3075	6	3259	0	3267
Richmondville	1666	21	2027	0	2023	12	2272
Schoharie	2588	11	2869	1	3090	2	3155
Seward	2203	-12	1925	1	1948	-13	1692
Sharon	2632	4	2716	1	2754	-6	2601
Summit	1800	5	1890	2	1924	-5	1818
Wright	1716	-3	1658	2	1717	-8	1588
County total	33548		33519		34469		33358

Source: Hough, 1867:xxxv.

by the Great Western Turnpike, a major "highway" built from Albany to Cherry Valley in 1802 and later extended to Syracuse and the Genesee Country of western New York State. The Village of Esperance, with a population of about 300 persons, was located on this major east-west route where the northward flowing Schoharie Creek was spanned by a covered toll bridge. With the exception of the 40-50 residents of Patchin Hollow (North Blenheim) the entire populace of the Town of Blenheim lived in dispersed farmsteads. Wright, the sixth town in the study area, was bisected east to west by a plank road connecting Albany and the Village of Schoharie. The Village of Gallupville, located approximately six miles east of the Village of Schoharie along the route of the plank road, was the only important settlement located within the Town of Wright.

Data Compilation

Data for this study were compiled from several nominal sources including the census manuscripts of 1855, 1860, and 1865, residential directories of 1860-1861 for selected cities, cemetery headstone inscriptions, and two newspapers published in the study area during the 1850s. These sources were manually combined to create a single, machine-readable file used in the statistical analyses.

The format and codebook of this file appear in Appendix C.

The most important of these data sources was the New York State manuscript census of 1855 for the six Schoharie County towns containing the sample population. This unusually rich, relatively untapped enumeration was the fourth of six decennial censuses conducted by the state beginning in 1825 (Middleton, 1905). The first three were much like those taken by the national government prior to 1850. They recorded little more than the name of the household head and the number of co-residing individuals of each gender and age group. In 1850 the census became for the first time a complete enumeration of the population. The name, age, gender, race, occupation, value of property owned and birthplace by country, or state or territory of the United States, was reported for each person.

The 1855 New York Census reported much of· this same information, as well as several other important characteristics of each person.(1) Relationship to the head of the census family was noted, as was the individual's current marital status, number of consecutive years residence in the town or city of enumeration, and, for natives of New York, county of birth. It also reported whether or not the person owned land, the literacy of persons aged 21 years or older, whether afflicted with a disability (blind, deaf, idiotic, etc.),

and if Negro, whether of not subject to taxes. The
building material and value of each occupied dwelling, a
potential surrogate for the socio-economic status of the
occupants, was also noted. A separate agricultural
schedule for each owner, operator, and tenant farmer
provided information about farm size, value, and
production. Nominal record linkage between these
schedules of the 1855 census permitted compilation of a
rather complete picture of most families in the study
area. (2)

Decomposition Techniques

Tracing the 11,922 people enumerated in the six
sample towns involved manual linkage of the 1855 file to
one or more of the following nominal record sources: the
1860 and 1865 census manuscripts, residential directories
for selected cities, cemetery records, and local newspaper
articles. Eleven steps were involved. These were as
follows:

1) Recapturing persisters by examining the 1860
census manuscripts of the sample towns,

2) Locating persisters not counted in the 1860
census by examining the 1865 census manuscripts of
the sample towns and examining the birthplaces of
their offspring born since 1855,

3) Recovering short-distance or partial
displacement migrants by examining the 1860 census
manuscripts of all towns adjacent to the sample
towns,

4) Compiling a directory of potential return migrants (family groups resident in the 1855 town of enumeration less than five years), identifying their places of residence in 1850, and searching the 1860 and 1865 census manuscripts of these places,

5) Identifying other intra-state migrants by examining the 1865 census manuscripts of non-sampled towns in Schoharie County and all towns in New York that reported an increase from 1855 to 1865 in the number of people born in Schoharie County,

6) Recovering long-distance intra-state migrants by examining the 1860 census manuscripts of towns not examined in step 2 but suggested by the places of residence determined in step 5,

7) Recapturing people identified in step 5 but not found using step 6 by examining the 1860 census manuscripts for places located between the places of residence in 1855 and 1865,

8) Recovering urbanward migrants by examining the 1865 census manuscripts for selected cities and consulting the 1860-1861 residential directories for these cities,

9) Identifying the potential long-distance destinations of inter-state migrants by comparing the distribution of people born in New York as enumerated in 1850 with that in 1860 and noting the places mentioned in local newspaper articles and records of church membership transfers,

10) Locating long-distance inter-state migrants by examining the 1860 census manuscripts for places suggested in step 9, and

11) Identifying those who died by examining headstone inscriptions, obituaries in the local newspapers, and noting missing people in recovered family groups.

The first step required alphabetization of the entire sample of 11,922 people by surname, preserving the integrity of each family group. I then examined the 1860 census manuscripts for each of the six sample towns. Linkage between the 1855 population "dictionary" was established by comparing names and personal attributes of individuals and of co-residents within each family group. I recovered an average of 60.8 percent of the sample using this method (Table 3.4) Differences in the rates of persistence between towns were not significant.(3)

I used the 1865 state census in the second step.(4) The census manuscripts of the sample towns were first searched to identify people who were probably missed by the census marshall in 1860.(5) Nearly 200 people were found in situ. Only one family, judging by the birthplace of a six year old child (Ulster County), had migrated before 1860 and subsequently returned. I then examined this same source for Schoharie's other ten towns and found 79 people who were intra-county migrants. It cannot be known with complete certainty that these 79, and 132 others found elsewhere in 1865 but not in 1860 using steps 4 and 5 below, migrated before and not after 1860 but I have assumed that mobility was constrained by the Civil War. Therefore, I included those found in 1865 but not in 1860 with either the persisters of 1860 or the migrants of

TABLE 3.4

PERSISTENCE IN SCHOHARIE COUNTY, 1855-1860

Town	N	Persisters	Rate
Blenheim	1348	802	59.50
Esperance	1370	839	61.24
Gilboa	2658	1576	59.29
Richmondville	2027	1254	61.86
Schoharie	2868	1743	60.77
Wright	1651	1030	62.39
	11922	7244	60.76

1860 as suggested by their place of residence in 1865 or by the birthplaces of their children.

Tracing Out-Migrants: Methods and Theory

Although social scientists and historians have developed several techniques for recovering persisters and analyzing in-migration, no satisfactory methods of tracing out-migrants have been developed. Knights (1971), in the first such effort, sought the whereabouts of those who left Boston during the ante-bellum period.(6) His quest led him to search the census manuscripts, vital records, genealogies, town histories, and directories of all 128 towns in Massachusetts. Of his original sample, 36 to 45 percent were recaptured within the city at the end of each of three decades (p. 105). An additional 9.1 to 12.7 percent were positively identified as out-migrants. Between 50 and 75 percent of these were found less than 10 miles from Boston (p. 113). He estimated that an untraced 30 percent left the state (p. 105).

Jensen, Stephenson, and Webster (1978) examined the mobility of individuals enumerated in the 1875 and 1905 New York and 1905 Wisconsin censuses. Using the SOUNDEX indexes to the censuses of 1880 and 1900 they recovered sixty percent of their original sample.(7) An average of 14 percent of this sample migrated, the overwhelming majority within the respective state. On the basis of their "obviously superior" methodology they concluded that the high rates of out-migration found by numerous other researchers are chimera (p. 236).

Their attempt to attribute the untraced 40 percent to mortality and problems with the census is, however, disturbing. They concede that more of the unfound may have been migrants than non-migrants, but seem unconcerned by the implications of in situ recovery rates that are not significantly different than those of other researchers. It may be conceptually weak of the "Thernstrom school" to define non-persisters as migrants and hence to conclude that transience was a hallmark of nineteenth century America, but it seems equally tenuous to conclude otherwise when only one-half of one's sample population can be identified as persisters. The usefulness of the SOUNDEX as an aid in tracing persisters and emigrants is clearly demonstrated, but further study is needed before wholesale revisions of contemporary thought about mobility during the nineteenth century are made.

Neither Knights (1971) nor Jensen et al. (1978) explicitly recognized that the new places of residence of those who emigrate from any given area are related to two factors: distance from the previous place of residence and residential experience of the individual and his acquaintances. The effect of distance, as modified by the

population size of the destination, is best summarized by
a gravity model. As elaborated by Zipf (1946), the amount
of interaction between two places is hypothesized to be
associated with the population size of those two places
and distance separating them. Large places at
considerable distance from one another would be expected
to have greater intercourse than two smaller places
separated by a like distance. Thus, Knights was correct
in beginning his search for Boston's non-persisters in the
adjacent towns of that city. However, he might have been
more successful in tracing those he did not find in these
towns had he consulted the nominal records of Hartford,
Albany, New York City, and Buffalo rather than those of
rural western Massachusetts. These large cities would,
given the gravity model, be expected to receive more
migrants from Boston than would less populated rural areas
of western Massachusetts.

The second factor is captured by the idea of
channelized migration flows. Research indicates that
migrants usually consider a small number of possible
destinations. These are of two types. The first type
includes prior places of residence, and return migration
to these is not unusual. Thistlewaite (1960) found that
during the late nineteenth and early twentieth centuries
one-third of all immigrants to the United States
subsequently returned to their European homelands. One

might reasonably expect that return migration within the United States would have been larger especially over short-distances. The second type of destination is based upon residence of friends and relatives at the intended destination. This is called the "migrant stock" hypothesis (Nelson, 1959; Greenwood, 1969). Importantly, these are sometimes destinations not predicted by the basic gravity model.

Intra-state Migrants

I applied a gravity model in step three and manually searched the census manuscripts for all towns contiguous to those in my sample area. The average distance from the center of each sample town to the center of each contiguous town was about seven miles. Approximately 40 percent of the non-persisters ultimately identified as out-migrants were recaptured with this proceudure.

The fourth step was predicated upon potential return migration. I first compiled a directory of all family groups containing individuals not born in Schoharie County. Special note was made of those families resident in their town of enumeration less than five years. I then located these families in the 1850 census by consulting the commerically produced census indexes to heads of households.(8) In instances of same-named entries I gave priority to the entry from the county closest to Schoharie or to that of the New York county of birth of a child between the ages of three and seven. These indexes provided the state, county, and town of residence in 1850 and the page number in the manuscript census of that year. I used this information as a clue to the whereabouts of out-migrants in 1860. Most people came from towns in one of six counties contiguous to Schoharie. I limited my search for possible return migrants to the 1860 and 1865 census manuscripts of these six counties, but almost every town was represented.

It was assummed in the fifth step that migrant stock, the previous migration of friends and relatives, was a factor in the choice of destinations by out-migrants. Published volumes of the censuses of 1855 (Hough, 1857) and 1865 (Hough, 1867) contain matrices of the town or city of residence on the date of enumeration by county of birth of New York natives. Thus, it was possible to compare the distribution of Schoharie-born persons in the two years (Fig. 3.3). Places that increased may have done so because of in-migration by members of the sample population. These places became targets for perusal of the 1860 census (Fig. 3.4).

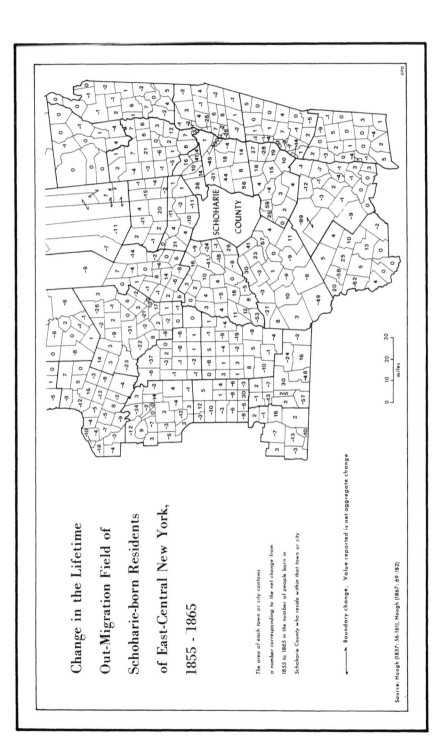

Change in the Lifetime Out-Migration Field of Schoharie-born Residents of East-Central New York, 1855 - 1865

The area of each town or city contains a number corresponding to the net change from 1855 to 1865 in the number of people born in Schoharie County who reside within that town or city

→ Boundary change. Value reported is net aggregate change

0   10   20   30
miles

Source: Hough (1857: 56.161), Hough (1867: 69:182)

Figure 3.3

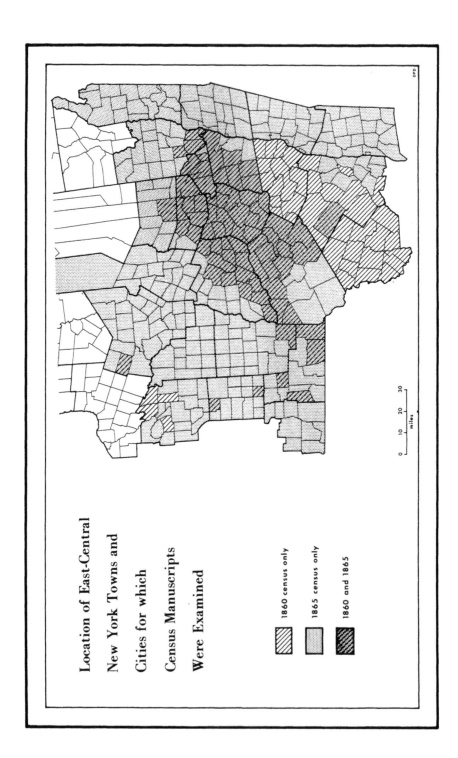

Location of East-Central
New York Towns and
Cities for which
Census Manuscripts
Were Examined

1860 census only

1865 census only

1860 and 1865

Figure 3.4

Searching the 1860 census manuscripts was narrowed to specific names by first examining the extant 1865 census manuscripts for the target areas.(9) This was rapidly accomplished by focusing on the place of birth column and checking the nominal entry for each person born in Schoharie County. Other characteristics including age and names of co-residing persons were then examined to determine if a match had been made. In the absence of such supporting evidence, I rejected the nominal match. In practice this resulted in exclusion of several common named individuals and most newlywed women.

At this stage, having traveled to the county seat or paid the rental fee for the microfilm copy, it was practical to examine the manuscripts for the entire county and not only the towns that showed an increase in the number of residents born in the county under study. A straight-forward net increase over a ten-year period takes into account neither mortality nor out-migration and replacement of either of these two by in-migrants, among whom might have been members of the sample population. This might very well be the case if a town had a relatively large number of residents from the study area in 1855 (Fig. 3.5) but declined only slighty in the ten years following. Given that recent migrants are more likely to chose as destinations the places containing

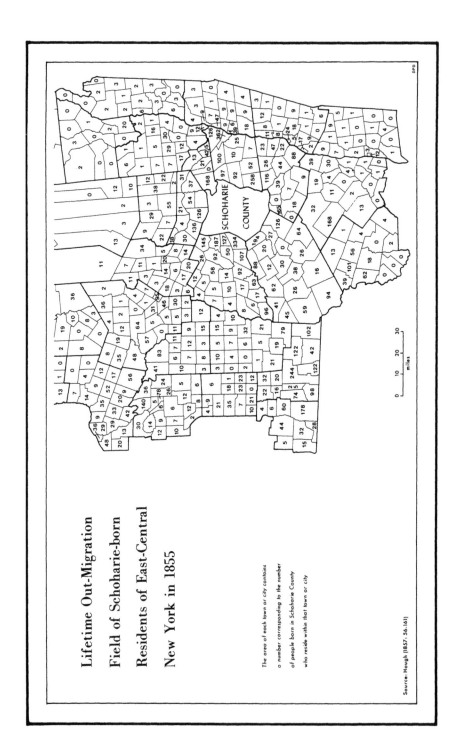

Lifetime Out-Migration Field of Schoharie-born Residents of East-Central New York in 1855

The area of each town or city contains a number corresponding to the number of people born in Schoharie County who reside within that town or city

Source: Hough (1857: 56-161)

Figure 3.5

friends who migrated previously, one may safely assert that the greater the number of migrants from the study area residing in a given town in 1855 the greater the likelihood of their replacement at death or out-migration by new in-migrants. Thus, there is a theoretical basis for examining the 1865 census manuscripts for towns not originally targeted by reason of a net increase in their population of residents born in Schoharie County.

Having recaptured a given individual in the 1865 census manuscript for a particular locale, I again consulted the 1860 census. Given a short list of names to match it was relatively quick and easy --- compared to the alternative of consulting my "dictionary" of nearly 4,000 non-persisters --- to locate out-migrants from the study area. I had much better success finding family groups than individuals, but this was expected. Individuals regularly exhibit greater mobility than family groups but I was also unwilling to accept as matches several same-named and same-aged persons. An uncommon occupation may assist in identifying the individual sought but barring some unusual characteristic the certainty of finding "John Smith, aged 18, occupation laborer" was a near impossibility. Most women who married and changed their surname were likewise not traceable.

People found in 1865 but not in 1860 were sought using a seventh step. If the place of residence in 1855 is viewed as one end point on a line segment and that in 1865 as the other, examination of the 1860 census manuscripts for places that fall along that segment may result in finding those people whose 1860 place of residence was different than that in 1865. Those people whose wherabouts are known in both 1855 and 1865 are likely in 1860 to have been somewhere along these routes.

Locating urbanward migrants was accomplished using an eighth step. In 1855 New York was one of the nation's most urbanized states. Nearly half of the Empire State's people lived in incorporated areas (Hough, 1857). A search for migrants from the sample towns using the 1865 census and follow-up 1860 method would require considerable effort. Consequently, I adopted a two stage abbreviated search strategy. I scanned the 1865 census by birthplace as described above for several cities but used residential directories for 1860-1861 and not the 1860 census for the follow-up. This method was advantageous because the directories are arranged alphabetically. It does, however, have two disadvantages. Directories tend to overlook recent in-migrants, lower class individuals, and non-white residents (Knights, 1969; Goldstein, 1954). They also exclude spouses and children from their listings. The latter was an inconsequential problem given linkage to the 1865 census that does include co-residents. To expedite the search for urbanward migrants I limited my quest to the nearby cities of Albany, Troy, Schenectady, Hudson, Poughkeepsie, Kingston, Binghamton, Utica, Rome, and Syracuse.

Inter-state Migrants

Longer-distance migrants, particularly those who left the Empire State, were located by examining the 1860 census manuscripts. Census indexes, church records, and the general news, letters to the editor, and notices of birth, death, and marriage published in Schoharie's two weekly newspapers were used as finding aids.

Initially I concerned myself with locating indexes to the 1860 censuses of states that experienced considerable increases from 1850 to 1860 in the number of residents born in New York state (Table 3.5). I found two of value. That for Minnesota is commerically produced and appears to be a complete surname index. The index for Wisconsin in 1860 includes every individual enumerated.(10) These were consulted, the county and manuscript census page number for each possible match noted, and the name in my "dictionary" of possible migrants checked against the manuscript census entry.

TABLE 3.5

THE DISTRIBUTION OF NEW YORK BORN,
BY STATE OR TERRITORY, 1850-1860

State	1850	1860	Increase
Michigan	133,756	191,128	57,372
Illinois	67,180	121,508	54,328
Wisconsin	68,595	120,637	52,042
Iowa	8,134	46,053	37,919
Minnesota	488	21,574	21,086
California	10,160	28,654	18,494
New Jersey	20,561	38,540	17,979
Pennsylvania	58,835	70,673	11,838
Missouri	5,040	14,585	9,545
Connecticut	14,416	22,614	8,198
Indiana	24,310	30,855	6,545
Kansas	-	6,331	6,331
Massachusetts	4,092	18,508	4,092
Colorado	-	3,942	3,942
Nebraska	-	2,322	2,322
Virginia	2,034	4,617	1,683
Texas	1,589	3,221	1,632
Tennessee	1,019	2,475	1,456
Vermont	2,881	4,170	1,289
Kentucky	2,881	4,170	1,289

Sources: Debow (1854);
         Population (1864);
         Report (1853).

Unfortunately, every state of interest is not indexed, and clues as to the new places of residence of emigrants had to be gleaned from church records reporting transfers of membership and from the pages of the local press. There were few of the former. Although pastors regularly indicated which members had requested a transfer they rarely noted where the person had gone. Moreover, considerably more women than men made such requests.

Newspapers proved to be a fruitful source of data. Two, the Schoharie Patriot and the Schoharie Republican were published weekly in Schoharie County throughout the 1850s, both at Village of Schoharie.(11) All of the extant issues of both papers for the period from January 1, 1850 through December 31, 1861 were read and particular attention given to mention of places outside Schoharie, especially those contained in letters to the editor, and in birth, death, and marriage notices (Table 3.6).

The two papers differed considerably in their opinions of prospects for emigrants to the West. Peter Mix, editor of the Patriot, consistently published articles that presented potential emigrants with bleak views of agriculture and commerce in the continent's interior. Farming was seen to be adversely affected by poorly drained soils, climatic extremes like unreliable rains and unseasonable frosts, and pests including locusts and rats. The prospects for those wishing to engage in

TABLE 3.6

SELECTED NON-NEW YORK PLACES IN THE SCHOHARIE PRESS (1)

Place	News	Letters	Notices of Birth	Mar.	Death
California		Rep			
Ca, Marysville	Pat				
Ca, La Grange				Rep	Pat
Ca, Oatvale					Rep
Ca, Spanish Flat		Rep			
Canada, Lancaster				Rep	
Ct, Collinsville	Rep				
Il, Belleville		Rep			
Il, Cook Co.		Rep			
Il, Kankakee	Rep				
Il, Lincoln					Rep
Il, Loda					Rep
Il, Mendota		Rep			
Il, Morris					Pat
Il, Richvieu Station		Rep			
Il, Rock Island		Pat,Rep			
Il, Starfield					Rep
Il, Sycamore					Rep
Il, Trivoli					Rep
Il, Winnebago					Pat
Il, Wyanet		Rep			
Indiana, Delphi					Rep
In, Rossville					Rep
Iowa, Anamosa	Rep				
Ia, Big Rock		Rep			
Ia, Burlington		Rep			
Ia, Camanche		Pat			
Ia, Council Bluff		Pat			
Ia, Decorah		Pat			
Ia, Dubuque		Pat			
Ia, Hawleyville	Pat				
Ia, Hopkinton		Rep			
Ia, Iowa Falls	Rep				
Ia, St. Charles City		Rep			
Ia, Smithland		Pat			
Ia, Tipton		Rep			

TABLE 3.6 (cont.)

Place	News	Letters	Notices of Birth	Mar.	Death
Kansas, Wyandott	Rep				
Michigan, Butler					Rep
Mi, Detroit		Rep			
Mi, Fayette				Rep	
Mi, Litchfield					Rep
Mi, Orien				Rep	
Minnesota	Rep				
Mn, Eyota					Rep
Mn, Mankato	Rep				
Mn, St. Paul	Rep	Rep			
New Jersey, Mendham		Rep			
NJ, N. Orange					Rep
NJ, Orange					Pat
Ohio, Painesville					Rep
Ohio, Urbana				Rep	
Pa, Great Bend		Rep			
Pa, New Milford					Rep
Pa, Wellsboro		Rep			Rep
Tennessee, Memphis					Rep
Utah, Fort Bridger	Rep				
Wisconsin, Racine	Pat				
Wi, Reedsburg		Rep		Rep	
Wi, Sauk City	Rep	Rep		Rep	
Wi, Sun Prairie	Rep				
Wi, Waukesha	Rep				
Wi, West Bend		Rep			
Wi, Weyauwega	Rep	Rep			
Wi, White Bend		Rep			

1 Published in issues of the Schoharie Patriot (Pat)
  and Schoharie Republican (Rep) dated January 1, 1855
  through December 30, 1860.

business and industry were also presented unfavorably. Rarely did a week pass that Mix did not comment on the high interest rates, bankruptcies, and recalled mortgages that had broken farmers and capitalists. His recommendation was for Schoharie's residents to stay put in the land they already knew rather than to pull-up stakes and risk all in the alien West.

The editors of the Republican were of a contrary opinion. Articles reprinted from western and New York papers lauded the richness of the soil, climate not unlike that of New York, bountiful harvests, and availability of land. Moreover, in contrast to Mix, the editors of the Republican encouraged their "western subscribers" to correspond with their friends and former neighbors in "Old Schoharie" through the pages of their newspaper (July 15, 1858). Many did so regularly and nearly all spoke favorably of the places they had visited and of their new homes in particular.

The datelines of these letters became guides to tracing emigrants in the sample population. After identifying the town(ship) and county in which each of these places was located I searched the 1860 manuscript census for people born in New York. For each such entry I checked the name in the census against those in my "dictionary" of non-persisters. I expected that migration to these places would be channelized and that finding one family would result in locating others. Surprisingly, this was not the case. I found only one family in addition to that of the letter writer, and in some cases the correspondent was not found.

The _Patriot_ and the _Republican_ also published birth, death, and marriage notices. I checked each of these notices in the issues dated from June, 1855 through December, 1861 against my "dictionary". The 1860 census manuscripts for the places mentioned in these notices were then perused for the names of other former residents of Schoharie. Only one such lead was rewarded. Eight families from the Town of Wright were found in Lincoln, Illinois, where the _Republican_ reported that two members of the Warner clan had died of typhoid fever (October 21, 1858; November 18, 1858).

The coverage of these two publications was not as exhaustive as I expected. First, the places related to these life-course events were not always mentioned. Second, any such event occurring to an emigrant would have required a letter from the person or his immediate kin. Many emigrants, having abandoned Schoharie, may not have felt the need to communicate with the community via the local press. Third, all notices were not published gratis. The _Republican_ made special mention of a 25 cent charge for marriage notices, leading me to suspect that it may also have exacted a fee for birth and death notices

(March 1, 1855). Fourth, there was little news from the southern part of the county. No improved roadway connected the Village of Schoharie, the place of publication of both newspapers, with settlements south of Patchin' Hollow, so it is quite likely that residents of Gilboa and other southern towns would have patronized the Prattsville Advocate in Greene County or the Bloomville Mirror, now the Stamford Mirror, in Delaware County.

Recapture Results

The steps thus far outlined led to a remarkably high recovery rate. The average persistence rate of 60.8 percent is considerably higher than that found in most studies of frontier and/or urban communities during the nineteenth century (see Tables 2.1 and 2.3). It is about one and one-half times greater than those of three roughly comparable areas. Barron (1980:109), in his study of Chelsea, Vermont, found twenty-year persistence rates of 32.1 percent and 34.3 percent for male heads of households for the years 1840-1860 and 1860-1880, respectively. Burton (1975:150) found that 43 percent of the residents of Edgefield County, South Carolina, persisted through the 1870s. The average decadal persistence rates from 1850-1880 among whites in Clarke County, Georgia, an area that included the city of Athens, was 42.6 percent (Huffman, 1974:35).

I also recovered a large percentage of the non-persisters (Table 3.7). Researchers working in other parts of New York should, with my method, now be able to more fully decompose their populations. Comparisons of persisters can now be made with known migrants and not with a heterogeneous group of non-persisters.

Mortality

In the introdution to this chapter, I indicated that previous researchers have not fully decomposed their sample populations. One aspect of this was in tracing out-migrants. In this section I discuss a second, identifying those who died.

To render my recovery rates comparable with those of Katz (1975) and Barron (1980), I adopted their strategy of using a model life table to estimate mortality (Table 3.8). The result was a significant improvement in the percentage of people located. Eighty-four percent of the estimated survivors are known to have either persisted or migrated.

Application of a model life table in this context assumes, however, that all those who died would have persisted had they survived. It is by no means

TABLE 3.7

RECOVERY OF THE SAMPLE POPULATION

(percentage)

| Town | N (1) | 1860 | | |
		Persisters	Migrants	Unknown
1. Blenheim	1348	802 (59.20)	246 (18.25)	300 (22.26)
2. Esperance	1370	839 (61.24)	179 (13.07)	352 (25.69)
3. Gilboa	2658	1576 (59.29)	407 (15.31)	675 (25.40)
4. Richmondville	2027	1254 (61.86)	309 (15.24)	464 (22.89)
5. Schoharie	2868	1743 (60.77)	384 (13.39)	741 (22.23)
6. Wright	1651	1030 (62.39)	254 (15.38)	367 (22.23)
Total	11922	7244 (60.76)	1779 (14.92)	2899 (24.32)

| Town | 1865 | | |
	Persisters	Migrants	Unknown
1. Blenheim	22 (1.63)	38 (2.82)	240 (17.80)
2. Esperance	27 (1.97)	21 (1.53)	304 (22.19)
3. Gilboa	57 (2.14)	41 (1.54)	627 (23.59)
4. Richmondville	11 (0.54)	45 (2.22)	408 (20.13)
5. Schoharie	59 (2.06)	46 (1.60)	636 (22.18)
6. Wright	22 (1.33)	21 (1.27)	324 (19.62)
Total	198 (1.66)	212 (1.78)	2539 (21.30)

1. Excludes five people who were enumerated twice.

TABLE 3.8
CONDITION OF THE POPULATION IN 1860
(percentage of survivors)

Town	N (1)	Survivors (2)	Persisters (3)
1. Blenheim	1348	1272	802 (63.05)
2. Esperance	1370	1286	839 (65.24)
3. Gilboa	2658	2513	1576 (62.71)
4. Richmondville	2027	1905	1254 (65.83)
5. Schoharie	2868	2704	1743 (64.46)
6. Wright	1651	1547	1030 (66.58)
Total	11922	11227	7244 (64.52)

Town	Migrants(3)	Unknown(3)	Persisters(4)	Migrants(4)	Unknown(4)
1.	246 (19.34)	224 (17.61)	22 (1.73)	38 (2.99)	164 (12.89)
2.	179 (13.07)	268 (20.84)	27 (2.10)	21 (1.63)	220 (17.11)
3.	407 (15.31)	539 (21.45)	57 (2.27)	41 (1.63)	432 (17.19)
4.	309 (16.22)	344 (18.06)	11 (0.58)	45 (2.36)	286 (15.01)
5.	384 (14.20)	582 (21.52)	59 (2.18)	46 (1.70)	472 (17.46)
6.	254 (16.42)	263 (17.00)	22 (1.42)	21 (1.36)	220 (14.22)
Total	1779 (15.85)	2220 (19.77)	198 (1.76)	212 (1.89)	1794 (15.98)

1 Excludes five people who were enumerated twice.
2 Estimated from Level 13 West, Coale and Demeny (1966). See Appendix D for breakdown by age cohort and gender for each town.
3 Status of survivors in 1860.
4 Status in 1865 of those classified as "Unknown" in 1860.

unreasonable to expect that some of the deceased would have migrated and then passed away. Rates of persistence actually range, then, somewhere between a rate unadjusted for mortality and one figured as above for complete in situ mortality.

In my sample from Schoharie County I determined actual mortality by consulting cemetery inscriptions (Barber, 1936), obituary notices in the county's two newspapers, and by comparing census family composition in 1855 and 1860. Moreover, the actual number of deaths was compared with the estimated mortality. Under enumeration of the former was attributed to mortality after migration.

The available sources of mortality data were incomplete, however. Not every cemetery was included in Barber's list of headstone inscriptions, and within those cemetaries that were surveyed some headstones were likely to be missing or illegible. Newspaper obituaries were also incomplete. It was obvious from the age distribution of these that deaths of children and the elderly were under-reported. So, too, were those occurring to poor, laboring class people and those in the southern part of the county. Some of these deaths could be inferred by comparing the names of family members in 1855 with those in 1860 but no such evidence was available for primary households or elderly couples who could not be recovered.

Recovery Biases

Decomposition of the sample population using the methodology above, although reasonably complete, was also biased. The persisting population is undoubtedly represented correctly but recovery of known emigrants was affected by nativity, gender, and age.

The methodology for tracing emigrants was based upon some member of the family group being born in Schoharie County. Scanning the 1865 census by birthplace missed all others. An emigrant recently arrived from Ireland, for example, could not be traced unless he or she parented a Schoharie-born child and that child was still living in 1865 with this parent. Likewise an elderly person born, for example, in Massachusetts may have emigrated to a nearby town but would not have been found unless residing with at least one Schoharie-born person.

The absence of complete marriage records militated against recovery of females who underwent surname changes. This affected those who married for the first time, probably a majority of the "unknown" between the ages of 15 and 30, and widows who remarried, an unknown percentage of those aged 15 to 60 (Fig. 3.6).

Males were more easily traced because they did not change surnames at marriage, but an age bias is again notable (Fig. 3.7). The proportion of "unknown" between

8

Figure 3.6

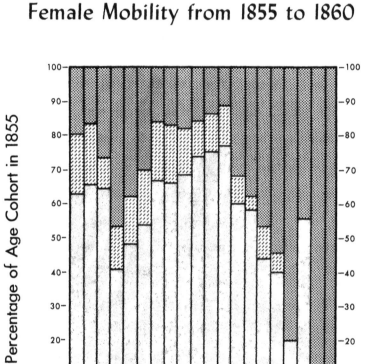

Female Mobility from 1855 to 1860

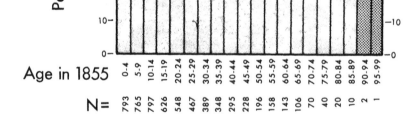

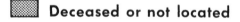
Deceased or not located

Out-Migrants

Non-Migrants

Figure 3.7

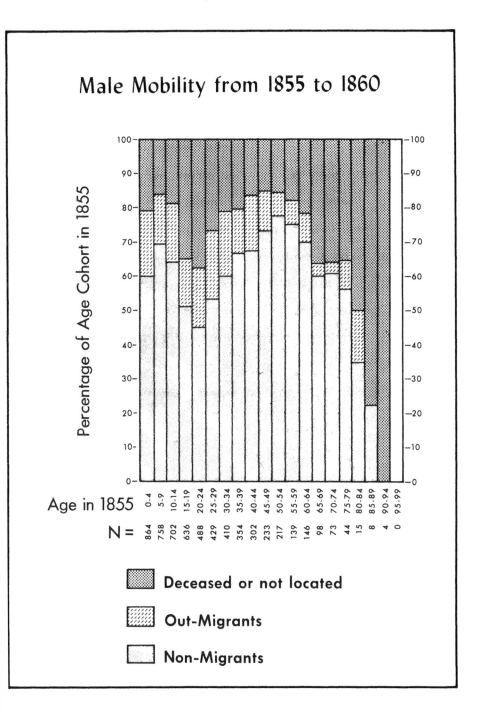

the ages of 15 and 30 is considerable, a probable indication, given the relatively low mortality expected among these cohorts, of the higher mobility of these individuals. However, it may also reflect the abnormal mortality experienced by these cohorts during the Civil War.

Mortality is probably the most important factor affecting recovery of unknown males and females aged 60+ (Fig. 3.8). Death records were, as noted above, incomplete, and I did not assign in situ mortality status to those for whom I have no records. An unknown number of the elderly, especially those without kin in Schoharie, may have migrated to previous places of residence or to the places of residence of their offspring before their death. The few obituaries that were published locally often indicated that the deceased passed away at the home of a son or daughter.

Male Headed Families

The recovery procedures discussed above were considerably more successful when applied to the 2,089 male heads of families enumerated in 1855.(12) More than 83 percent of the male heads of families were identified in 1860 as either persisters or migrants (Table 3.9). Another 3.65 percent, still living in 1865, were

Figure 3.0

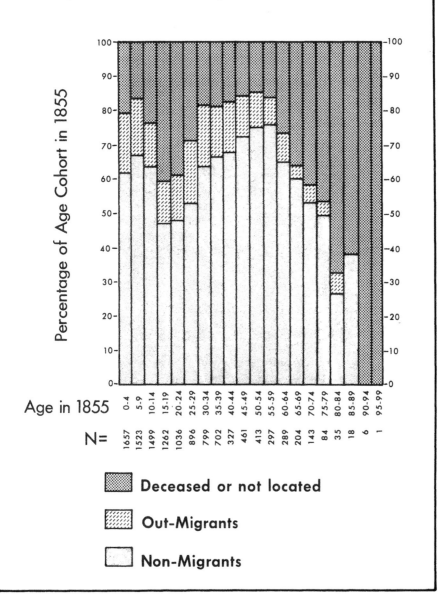

Population Mobility from 1855 to 1860

TABLE 3.9

STATUS OF MALE HEADS OF FAMILIES IN 1860/65

(percentage)

Age	N	1860			1865		
		Non-Mig.	Mig.	Unkn.	Non-Mig.	Mig.	Unkn.
15-19	2	2	0	0	0	0	0
20-24	89	48	17	24	4	5	15
25-29	265	155	64	46	8	9	29
30-34	327	199	79	49	8	8	33
35-39	312	210	48	54	3	5	46
40-44	269	182	54	33	5	2	26
45-49	213	161	27	25	2	2	21
50-54	197	156	16	25	3	3	19
55-59	124	98	9	17	2	1	14
60-64	121	95	8	18	1	0	17
65-69	78	50	2	26	0	2	24
70-74	54	38	1	15	1	1	13
75-79	27	18	2	7	0	1	6
80+	11	5	0	6	0	0	6
	2089	1417	327	345	37	39	269
	(100)	(67.83)	(15.65)	(16.52)	(1.78)	(1.87)	(12.88)

presumably missed in the 1860 census. The remaining 13 percent who were not traced either died or migrated. Since the decision to migrate undoubtedly was made by the family head the detailed analyses of differentials presented in chapters 4 and 5 focus on the socio-demographic and economic characteristics of this sub-group of the population and their families.

A sizeable proportion of the male heads of families not found were elderly and probably died (Fig. 3.9). In this respect, the mortality records derived from cemetery inscriptions, newspaper obituaries, and census family comparisons were more complete than they had been for the entire population. Forty percent of the 269 male heads of families not located in either 1860 or 1865 are known to have died in situ before 1860 (Table 3.10). These 112 constitute 60 percent of those expected to die between 1855 and 1860. Moreover, this percentage is nearly the same as that for the number of persisters known to be living in 1860. The other 40 percent estimated to have died between 1855 and 1860 probably did so after migrating. This hypothesis is further supported by the figures for survivorship by cohort. The number of known dead in the younger cohorts is smaller in relation to the number of "unknown" than in the older cohorts.

Figure 3.9

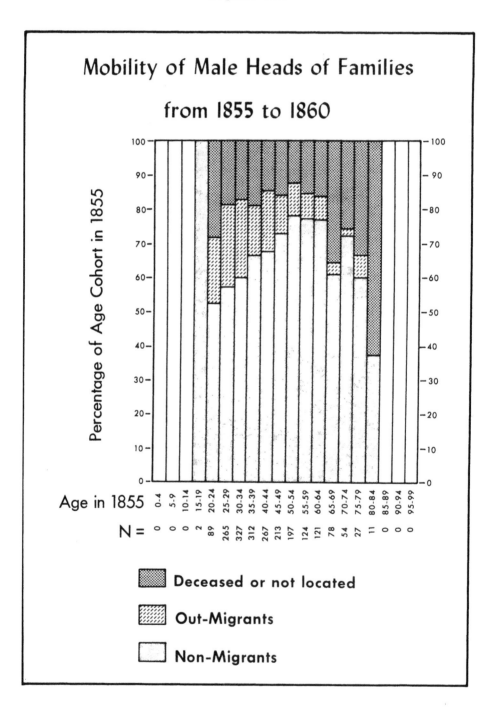

Mobility of Male Heads of Families from 1855 to 1860

TABLE 3.10

MORTALITY OF MALE HEADS OF FAMILIES (1)

Age	Unknown(2)	Est. Deaths(3)	Known Dead(4)	Migrants
15-19	0	0.00	0	0
20-24	15	2.77	2	13
25-29	29	9.04	4	25
30-34	33	12.20	8	25
35-39	46	14.49	10	36
40-44	26	15.47	9	17
45-49	21	15.17	7	14
50-54	19	18.60	9	10
55-59	14	15.46	8	6
60-64	17	21.15	10	7
65-69	24	18.78	21	3
70-74	13	18.13	12	1
75-79	6	12.54	6	0
80+	6	11.00	6	0
	269	184.8	112	157

1 Breakdown by town is found in Appendix E.

2 Not located in either 1860 or 1865 and presumed to have either died in situ or migrated.

3 Estimated from Level 13 West, Coale and Demeny (1960).

4 Determined from cemetary headstone inscriptions (Barber, 1936), obituaries published in the Schoharie Patriot and Schoharie Republican, and widows and parentless children enumerated in the 1860 census manuscripts. Includes two known migrants who died at their new places of residence before the census of 1860.

5 The unknowns minus the known dead.

In subsequent analyses I excluded the 110 heads of families who died _in situ_ and were not at risk to either persist through 1860 or migrate. The 73 others who probably died after migrating are retained in the sample because they exhibited the behavior being studied. The final sample consists, then, of 1,454 male heads of families who persisted and 525 male heads of families who out-migrated (Table 3.11).

Summary

Given the quality of historical nominal records, decomposition of any population is a difficult task. No single source readily identifies out-migrants and previous studies have not applied a theoretically based search strategy to exhaust the nominal data sources available. The effect of mortality has been taken into account when figuring persistence rates, but estimates of mortality have not been compared with actual figures to differentiate _in situ_ deaths from those occurring after migration.

The methodology presented in this chapter demonstrates that census manuscripts, newspaper articles, church records, and cemetery inscriptions can be searched using a strategy grounded in theory, and that male heads

TABLE 3.11

RECOVERY OF MALE HEADS OF FAMILIES, 1855-1860
(percentage)

Age	N (1)	Persisters	Known Migrants	Assumed Migrants
15-19	2	2 (100.0)	0 (0.0)	0 (0.0)
20-24	52	52 (59.77)	22 (25.29)	13 (14.94)
25-29	262	163 (62.21)	74 (28.24)	25 (9.54)
30-34	319	207 (64.89)	87 (27.27)	25 (7.84)
35-39	303	213 (70.30)	54 (17.82)	36 (11.88)
40-44	260	187 (71.92)	56 (21.54)	17 (6.54)
45-49	206	163 (79.13)	29 (14.08)	14 (6.80)
50-54	188	159 (84.57)	19 (10.11)	10 (5.32)
55-59	116	100 (86.21)	10 (8.62)	6 (5.17)
60-64	111	96 (86.49)	8 (7.21)	7 (6.31)
65-69	57	50 (87.72)	4 (7.02)	3 (5.26)
70-74	42	39 (92.86)	2 (4.76)	1 (2.38)
75-79	21	18 (85.71)	3 (14.29)	0 (0.00)
80+	5	5 (100.0)	0 (0.00)	0 (0.00)
	1979	1454 (73.47)	368 (18.60)	157 (7.93)

1. Total enumerated in 1855 minus those who died _in situ_.

of families, the probable migration decision makers, can be fully decomposed with confidence.

Notes

1. Age was reported to the nearest year for people one or more years of age. Age in months was reported for those under one year of age. The age distribution among adults suggests a slight tendency toward "heaping" at years ending in zero. Marital status was based on whether or not the individual was currently married. A mark in the space provided on the census manuscript indicated an affirmative response, but one should not assume that a blank meant "single and never married." Some census takers wrote "w" or "d" to indicate widowed and divorced, respectively, but they received no instructions to do so. This clarification may be of some importance. One should not assume, for example, that an unmarried mother had her child out of wedlock or that an unmarried fifty year old woman had never married. Both may have been widows. Duration of residence was given in years in response to the question concerning "consecutive years residence in this city or town." The responses of an extremely small number of people, many of whom may have been return migrants, were deemed missing because inconsistencies exist in the responses of family members. William Chilson, for example, answered twenty years to this question but his three year old son, James, was born in Wisconsin. Apparently William and others reported cummulative and not consecutive years residence. Landownership was recorded as yes or no. Race was indicated as blank (white), black, or mulatto. There were no Orientals or Indians in Schoharie County. Nativity was reported by county for those born in New York State, state or territory for other states of the Union (occassionally a specific city or county was mentioned), and foreign country. Individuals who gave the same answer to the questions for age and duration of residence were deemed natives of the town where enumerated. Judgement as to the value of each dwelling was made by the census taker on the basis of his estimate of the market value in 1855 "without reference to assessed value or original cost" (New York, Secretary of State, 1855). Since census marshalls were not trained real estate appraisers, comparisons of the values assigned in one place may not be comparable with

those made by a different census taker in another. This mitigates against use of this variable in studies that sample from geographically dispersed locales. Moreover, the census taker was instructed to include the value of the house lot in making his assessment of dwellings located in villages and cities but not to do so for dwellings in the countryside. This suggests that use of this variable as a comparative measure of housing quality, etc. between urban and rural residents is inappropriate.

2. All of the nominal record linkage in this research was done manually. Machine-readable census files for the possible destinations of emigrants do not exist, and since I did not have research assistants to compile these I chose the most expedient process. However, I did short-cut data entry by eliminating manual coding and key-punching. Instead, I placed a CRT and microfilm reader next to each other and entered data on a computer disk file interactively.

3. In this small sample of six towns there appears to be no correlation between persistence rates and the percentage of population change between 1855 and 1860 (see Tables 3.3 and 3.4).

4. The manuscripts that have survived are available in two have survived are available in two forms. The original bound volumes are usually located in the office of the Clerk of the respective counties (those for Oneida County are housed at the Utica Public Library). A second and potentially more accessible source is the collection of the Genealogical Society of Utah. Most, but not all, of the 1865 manuscript census, as well as those for many other years, are available on microfilm at their branch libraries located in LDS Churches throughout the country. These must be used on the library premises but I did secure permission to install a phone line for use with a portable computer terminal.

5. Knights (1971:147) estimates that between 7 and 10 percent of Boston's residents were not enumerated in the 1850 and 1860 censuses.

6. In a more recent effort Peter Knights is attempting to reconstruct the life histories of 2,808 men who resided in Boston in 1860 or 1870. Thus far he has completed work for 96 percent of them (Knights, 1982).

7. The SOUNDEX is a phonetic-based indexing system. Surnames are alphabetized by first letter and succeeding consonants are grouped by sound and numerically coded. The SOUNDEX to the 1880 census includes only heads of

households containing children 10 years of age and younger and persons with surnames differing from that of the head of the household. It does not include, for example, single-member households and married couples without children. It would include a "boarder or servant" only when the household also contained a child age 0 - 10. The 1900 SOUNDEX contains all heads of households and co-residing different surnamed people. Use of the SOUNDEX is discussed by Stephenson (1980a).

8. The largest commercial enterprise specializing in indexing is Accelerated Indexing, Inc. of Salt Lake City, Utah. Their catalogue includes most states through 1850 but only scattered coverage of more recent censuses. Moreover, they usually index only heads of households. The apparently complete indexing of Minnesota in 1860 is not customary. Failure to index every person, an admittedly monumental task, virtually precludes retrospective tracing of newly formed families. For those who wish to do so I recommend application of a gravity model.

9. The manuscript census of 1865 for several potentially important towns in Greene, Oneida, Onondaga, and Ulster counties are missing or illegible, so I went directly to the 1860 census manuscripts for these places and used the tiresome name by name method.

10. The complete surname index for Wisconsin in 1860 and 1870 is held by the State Historical Library in Madison. This was compiled during the 1930s by employees of the WPA. A 16mm microfilm copy is available for inter-library loan.

11. The Patriot, with a circulation of 400, was the unofficial organ of the county's Whig Party and, from 1857 onward the Republican Party. Its editor and publisher, Peter Mix, an advocate of persistence, was a native of Dutchess County, New York who arrived in the Town of Schoharie in 1827 at the age of thirty-six. The Republican, with a circulation of 800, was the unofficial organ of the county's Democratic Party. Its half dozen editors and publishers encouraged Schoharie's residents to leave the area and some took their own advice. William Gallup, a native of Albany County, arrived in Schoharie in 1830 at the age of 18. He acquired the Republican in the mid 1840s after his Helderberg Advocate, an anti-rent newspaper, ceased publication. In April, 1853 he entered into partnership with J. B. Hall, a 25 year old printer from Wellsboro, Pennsylvania but editorial differences caused Hall to leave in October, 1854. The latter

established the Cobleskill Sentinel in a nearby town and Gallup shortly thereafter sold the Republican to Nathan Rossetter of nearby Middleburgh. Gallup traveled in the Mid-West during January and February of 1856 and eventually migrated with his family to Leyden Center, Cook County, Illinois. There he served as Justice of the Peace until his death from scarlet fever in 1863. Hall and Rossetter merged their publications in December, 1854 and briefly renamed the paper the Democratic Republican in an effort to clearly identify the political preferences of the editors. Hall left in 1859 and became publisher of the Catskill Journal in nearby Greene County. Rossetter, a retired judge and owner of Middleburgh's "Rossetter House", one of county's premiere inns, soon thereafter sold the Republican to Jeremiah Campbell, who subsequently moved to Schoharie from Cobleskill.

12. One hundred and fifty-six families were headed by women and nearly all were widows. These were not included in the analyses of differentials because they were a relatively homogeneous group. Most were over fifty years of age and had no occupation.

CHAPTER 4

MIGRATION DIFFERENTIALS

Previous studies of population redistribution within the United States during the 1800s have not been explicitly concerned with migration differentials. The characteristics of in-migrants have been examined and the socio-demographic and economic differences between persisters and non-persisters investigated, but no work has systematically decomposed the population of a given locale and directly compared the characteristics of non-migrants with those of out-migrants. Conclusions thus far reached about migration selectivity during the nineteenth nineteenth century are, therefore, only suggestive.

This chapter focuses on differences in the socio-demographic and economic characteristics between those who migrated from the study area and those who did not. It consists of two major parts. The first is a review of the expected differences between migrants and non-migrants as suggested in existing theoretical and empirical literature. The second tests a model of hypothesized differences between migrants and non-migrants using the sample of 1979 male heads of families at risk as identified in Chapter 3. Two levels of analyses are presented. The first is bivariate. Chi-square and student's t-test are utilized on categorical and interval scale attributes of the sample population, respectively. The second level of analysis is multivariate. Multiple Classification Analysis (MCA) is used to explore the relationships between explanatory variables and express the relative strength of each in predicting propensity to migrate. Two such analyses are presented. The first investigates the entire sample population. The second examines behavior by landowning farmers.

Factors Affecting Mobility

Residents of Schoharie County, New York, in 1855 were undoubtedly confronted with "push and pull" factors similar to those faced by most residents of rural areas throughout antebellum New York and New England. Farmers had to contend with decreasing crop yields, western competition, and labor shortages that encouraged use of machinery of limited value to side-hill farmers. Farmer and non-farmer alike may have recognized that the county's high population density (54 persons per square mile), lack of undeveloped soils, and relative isolation severely limited the economic opportunities of the populace.

Many people probably weighed these factors and others in assessing the "place utility" (Wolpert, 1965) of Schoharie in relation to alternative places of residence. Nearby cities and virgin farmlands in the West may have been foremost among these. A rapidly improving transportation system in the northeastern United States encouraged centralization of manufacturing in cities. Schoharie's residents explored the extent to which their skills may have been marketable in these centers of industry and commerce. So, too, were they probably informed of prospects for betterment in recently settled and frontier lands in the West by friends and relatives who had migrated previously. Untilled prairie could be acquired for a pittance of its potential value and non-farmers undoubtedly recognized that as land was alienated farmers would require their products and services. The opportunites available in cities and on the frontier must have been very attractive compared to those of most rural areas of the northeastern United States during the mid nineteenth century.

The migration decisions made by heads of families in Schoharie County and other rural areas of the Northeast were undoubtedly affected by life-cycle factors, place ties, economic conditions, and other socio-demographic characteristics of each potential migrant. These groupings of attributes encompass the significant migration differentials regularly observed in other studies. (Mangalam, 1968; Price and Sikes, 1975; Shaw, 1975; Thomas, 1938). The specific differentials so categorized include the following. Age, marital status, and family size are associated with an individual's life-cycle (Lee, 1970:297). Duration of residence, prior migration experience, kinship ties, and ownership of land are collectively termed place ties or, as they are called by DeVanzo (1976), location specific capital. Occupation, socio-economic status or rank, and the value of property occupied indicate one's economic condition. Race and national origin are within a fourth group of undifferentiated socio-demographic attributes.

Life-cycle

Life-cycle characteristics consistently have been important migration correlates. Key events, many of them occurring in one's late teens and twenties, are closely associated with migration. Early in an individual's life one is likely to migrate as part of a family group. The addition of siblings often results in migration to a more commodious dwelling. Later, as one reaches late adolescence, societal pressures to wed and leave the parental home, or to secure employment depart increase. The earlier cycle of seeking appropriate housing is repeated as the wedded individual procreates. When old-age approaches one may consider moving to a smaller, more easily cared for home or joining the family of one's son or daughter.(1)

Age is the most important life-cycle correlate of migration (Deutschman, 1972; Speare, 1970; Thomas, 1938). Young children and young adults are more likely to migrate than others in the population. The former often is associated with migration by recently enlarged families seeking more commodious housing. The latter is related to leaving the parental home and establishing one's own family, key life-cycle events that occur for most people in their late teens or twenties (Wall, 1978). E. G. Ravenstein, the first student of migration, observed (1876:230) that "most migrants are adults" but his data sources, the 1851 and 1861 censuses of Great Britain, were inadequate for detailed analysis by cohort. Thomas summarized the findings of several researchers and concluded (1938:11) that:

> There is an excess of adolescents and young adults among migrants, particularly migrants from rural areas to towns, compared with the non-migrants or the general population.

Studies by historians of the nineteenth century also indicate a relationship between age and persistence. Griffen and Griffen (1978:18) found that young, single boarders were less persistent than others in Poughkeepsie.

Barron (1980:113) likewise found among male residents of Chelsea, Vermont, that those aged 30 or more were one and one-half times more likely to persist than those less than 30 years of age.

It is also well established that marital status is an important life-cycle migration correlate. (Hollingsworth, 1970; Taeuber et al., 1968). Unmarried people are more mobile than married people of the same age. Those who are single are probably more independent and certainly have fewer factors to consider when deciding whether or not to move. The "family man" must consider the type of housing available, schooling for his children, and whether or not income potential will be adequate for the family. The individual does not act under these same constraints. Unless bound by apprenticeship, he is free to act in his self-interest and move whenever the urge strikes. Moreover, those who are members of family groups may be encouraged to "make room" for younger siblings and to seek employment and residence outside the parentally headed household.

Family size, a third life-cycle factor, may also be an important migration correlate (Long, 1973). Two families alike in all respects except the number of children may be expected to differ in their migration behavior. The larger of these two should exhibit greater mobility as pressures mount to lessen crowding. This

might be particularly true in a comparison of families
with young children. In general, procreating families are
probably more mobile than completed families.

Place ties

Migration is closely associated with a set of
factors collectively termed place ties. These include
such attributes as prior migration experience, duration of
residence, the presence of relatives, and ownership of
property. Each of these variables is an "investment" in a
given place that focuses the decision to migrate upon
those places to which one has ties. People born at or
resident for several years at their current locale, who
have relatives there, and who own their present home or
other real estate, are not likely to migrate. Conversely,
those who possess opposing attributes are likely to leave.

Prior migration experience is also closely
associated with one's propensity to migrate. Lifetime
residents of any given place have not acquired experience
in other places of residence that would provide a
comparative basis for evaluation of place utilities.
Conversely, people who have resided elsewhere can make as
many such comparisons as warranted by the number of
previous places of residence. Factors that in-migrants
find important in their subsequent decision to out-migrate

may not have occurred to natives simply because natives had no first-hand knowledge of conditions elsewhere. Moreover, chronic movers are more likely to migrate again than are infrequent movers and natives (Morrison, 1970). People who have moved several times seldom live anywhere very long. Morrison found that only 4.2 percent of those persons who had not moved in the last eight years did so in the ninth. Conversely, 70 percent of those who had moved eight times in eight years also moved in the ninth.

Duration of residence has an important effect on migration behavior. Recently-arrived inhabitants of a given place are considerably more likely to emigrate from that place than are long-time residents and natives of the place. This observation is best explained by the "axiom of cumulative inertia" (Myers et al., 1967). The longer one is a resident in a given place the more likely one is to acquire place ties that constrain out-migration. The relationship between duration of residence and propensity to migrate is not linear, however. Research indicates that a disproportionate number of out-migrants usually arrived in that place within the past three years (Goldstein, 1958). There is little difference in the migration behavior of those resident five years in comparison with ten or twenty year residents.

The number of friends and relatives in a given locale have an important effect upon the decision to migrate. People who belong to voluntary associations like a a church, service clubs, etc. are less likely to leave than are those who have not joined such groups. Moreover, members of spatially close kinship networks are, according to Johnston (1971:17), "much more resistant to the migration idea than [are] those with no such ties." He found in his study of rural Yorkshire, England, that fewer than half of the 5,149 adults drawn from the 1962 Electoral Registers had been residents of the same districts in 1951, but of those with common surnames, two-thirds were resident in the same district in 1951. Moreover, his analysis showed that different migration rates were a function of the relative size of the kinship network. Those districts with the greatest concentration of common surname groups were also those with the highest rates of population stability.

Bieder (1973:429) found that kinship ties among residents of Benzonia, Michigan, "functioned . . . persuasively in curbing out-migration" from 1857 through 1890. Families with kinship ties in 1864 were nearly three times more likely to be present through 1885 than were families without nearby relatives. Moreover, predominantly endogamous marriage patterns and preference for kin in employment "resulted in extended households, a solution which kinship ties made possible and which produced a kind of ´clannishness´ still evident in Benzonia today" (p. 438).

Ownership of real property also is an important predictor of migration behavior. Lansing and Mueller (1967) found that 70 percent of those who had not moved during the preceeding five years either owned or were buying a home. Only 30 percent of the non-homeowners had not moved during the same period. Likewise, Deutschman (1972) found that renters were twice as likely to move as homeowners.

Studies of the nineteenth century have also identified property ownership as an important migration differential. Manring (1978:408-409) found that those without property departed Nodaway County, Missouri, during the 1850s in much larger numbers than those owning real estate. Griffen (1969:59) found that "those without property left [Poughkeepsie] much more frequently." Worthman (1971:186) found that regardless of race and occupation "proportionately more property owners than propertyless workers remained in [Birmingham] for a decade." Thernstrom and Knights (1971:36) noted that men without property were from two to five times more likely to leave Boston than men with property. Katz (1975:131) observed that persisters in Hamilton, Ontario were two and one-half times more likely to own their homes than were non-persisters. Moreover, he concluded (p. 132) that:

> Clearly, home ownership exerted more influence on persistence than any other factor. In fact, it was in some senses equivalent, for undoubtedly the decision to buy a house very often represented a commitment to remain within the city.

Economic factors

The relationship between migration and occupation, as an indicator of income potential and status, is clearly suggested by existing studies. People in higher status occupations tend to migrate with greater frequency than do those in lower status jobs. Richmond (1969) and Tilly (1974) indicate that this is a function of the labor market. The supply and demand for higher skilled workers is more likely to extend beyond local to regional and national levels than is that for lesser skilled workers. This finding is supported by the work of Tarver (1964) and Miller (1965), who noted that people engaged in professional and technical occupations are twice as mobile as others. Friedlander and Rosheir (1966), likewise, found that only 18.5 percent of those engaged in the professions were life-long residents of their study area compared with 47.8 percent of the unskilled manual laborers.

Studies of occupation and mobility in nineteenth century cities have concluded otherwise. Although relevant studies were few, Thernstrom and Knights (1971:32) tentatively concluded that "men on the lower rungs of the class ladder were less rooted, not more rooted, than their betters." Blue collar workers have been found to possess appreciably greater mobility than white collar workers, but unskilled and semi-skilled laborers are the most mobile of all occupational groups. This argument is supported by the findings of Chudacoff (1972), Engerman (1975), Griffen (1969), and Hopkins (1968). Thernstrom (1973:30-38) contends that the higher rates of migration of professionals and other high-status, white-collar workers found in studies of the twentieth century are a relatively recent development associated with modernization of the country's economic structure. The norm in nineteenth century cities was high persistence among the upper classes.

Persistence studies conducted by rural historians also establish the importance of occupation as an indicator of one's propensity to migrate. Malin (1935) found that people employed in non-farm occupations in a rural Kansas township were more likely to migrate than those engaged in farming. Bowers (1960) found that during the period from 1850 to 1870 the turnover of population in a rural Iowa township was higher among non-farm occupations than among farmers, but conceeded that his sample size was too small to be significant. Curti (1959:69) found remarkably high turnover for both farmers and non-farmers in his study of mid-nineteenth century Trempealeau County, Wisconsin, with a slightly higher percentage of the non-farm population leaving.

The value of property is also an economic factor affecting migration behavior. Manring (1978:409) and Thorne (1959:320) both found that geographic mobility is inversely related to farm size. Bowers (1960:22-23) found that among both farm and non-farm populations 80 percent of those owning real estate valued at less than $500 left the study area but only 50 percent of those owning property valued at more than $500 did so. Thernstrom and Knights (1971:36) found that those owning property valued at less than $200 had an equal probability of leaving or staying but that mobility decreased thereafter with increased property value. The very wealthy, those with property valued at more than $10,000, were four to six times more likely to remain in Boston than to migrate.

Other socio-demographic factors

Race also may be an important migration differential. Contemporary scholars have found that non-whites are less mobile than whites (Lansing and Mueller, 1967) but Griffen and Griffen (1978:25) found the opposite to be true of 20-29 year old males in Poughkeepsie from 1870 to 1880. The low persistence rate for Blacks was, according to these scholars, "not explained by differences in skill distribution" (p. 31). Blacks had long occupied the lowest rung on the city's ladder of socio-economic status. They were materially Poughkeepsie's poorest residents, a fact attested to by their disproportionate representation at the Alms House. Griffen and Griffen concluded (p. 31) that:

> neither public policy nor private employment gave
> the city's blacks, many of them from families
> resident in the Hudson Valley for generations, any
> reason to look upon [Poughkeepsie] or any
> neighboring community as a place of opportunity
> for themselves or their children.

The differences in mobility of native-born Americans and immigrants groups also have been of particular interest to social historians of the nineteenth century. Blumin (1976:95), for example, found that after three years of residence in Kingston, New York the foreign-born component of that town's population enumerated in 1855 was twice as likely not to be found in

Kingston's 1860 census as were people born in the United
States but not in Ulster County, where Kingston is
located. Comparable findings of higher migration rates
among immigrants also have been made for other North
American cities during the nineteenth century. However,
Katz (1975) found in his study of Hamilton, Ontario, that
national origin was highly correlated with other, more
important, factors, and that these and not national origin
alone were responsible for the observed differences in
mobility. He concluded (p. 127) that:

> All ethnic groups, it is abundantly clear, were on
> the move to a roughly similar extent. . . .
> undoubtedly their wealth, rather than any
> independent cultural factor, most often accounted
> for the small ethnic differential in the tendency
> to remain within the city.

Evidence for rural areas is rather sparse.
Manring (1978:405-406) found in his study of Nodaway
County, Missouri, that the greatest proportion of
persisters from 1860 to 1870 were natives of Missouri or
adjacent states and that propensity to migrate was closely
associated with distance from state of birth. Curti
(1959:72-72) concluded in his study of Trempealeau County,
Wisconsin, 1850-1880, that the foreign born demonstrated
greater mobility than native born Americans and that among
the former non-English speakers evinced greater mobility
than English speaking immigrants. Barron (1980)
differentiated the 317 males aged 20-49 in Chelsea,

Vermont, in 1860 by national origin and observed that the Irish were nearly three times more likely to persist to 1870 than non-Vermonters born in the United States (p. 120). However, his sample sizes were only seven and forty-three, respectively.

Migration: Bivariate Analysis of the Sample

The population at risk consisted of 1,979 male heads of families. The 1,454 who did not change their town of residence from 1855 to 1860 or 1865, were classified as persisters/non-migrants. The 368 known migrants and 157 assumed migrants were together classified as out-migrants. Differences in the personal and family attributes of members of these two groups were first examined using bivariate statistical tests. Chi-square was used for categorical variables. Student's t-test was employed for interval scale variables. A significance level of .05 was adopted for both tests.

The variables tested were of five "types". These included: 1) variables used as reported in the population schedule of the 1855 New York State Census, 2) variables computed from data reported in the latter source, 3) variables used as reported in the agricultural schedule of the 1855 census, 4) variables computed from data reported in the latter source, and 5) variables used as reported in the population schedule of the 1860 national census.

Those of the first type included age, marital status, duration of residence, landownership, race, and nativity by country, state of the United States, and county of New York. The following are type two variables. Family size and the number of children aged 0-4 years are simple counts of co-residing individuals. The size of kinship groups was determined by counting the number of same surnamed persons and heads residing within the town of enumeration.(2) Each occupation initially received a unique code. These were collapsed subsequently into five meaningful categories, and a sixth for those who reported no occupation (Appendix F). Economic rank was found for each family group by dividing family size by the total number of people residing in each dwelling and multiplying this fraction by the value of the dwelling (Katz et al., 1978). Residents of "insitutional" dwellings including hotels, boarding houses, mill dormitories, school residence halls, and the county jail were excluded from analyses using economic rank.

Five variables in the agricultural schedules of the 1855 census, including the dollar value of farm land, dollar value of livestock, dollar value of agricultural implements, improved farm acreage, and unimproved farm acreage, were tested as reported.

Type four variables were calculated as follows: 1) total dollar value of the farm, the sum of the value of farm land, livestock, and agricultural implements; 2) total farm acreage, the sum of improved acreage and unimproved acreage; 3) percent improved acreage, improved acreage divided by total acreage; and 4) dollar value per acre, the value of farm land divided by total acreage.

Two variables from the 1860 manuscript census constitute the fifth type. These were dollar values of real estate and personal estate. However, on the assumption that a blank was as likely to mean no value given as zero, only those people with actual values greater than zero reported were included in subsequent analyses of these variables.

Life-cycle

Most attributes of out-migrants were, as hypothesized, significantly different from those of non-migrants (Table 4.1). Out-migrants were younger than non-migrants. This suggests that out-migrants were at an earlier stage in their life-cycles. However, the age differential was not as great as expected. Non-migrants were, as anticipated, middle-aged but out-migrants should have been in their middle to late twenties. Instead, the average age of an out-migrant was 37, only six years fewer

TABLE 4.1

BIVARIATE ANALYSES OF DIFFERENTIALS BETWEEN NON-MIGRANTS AND OUT-MIGRANTS

CHARACTERISTIC	N	TEST	X2	MEANS NON-MIGR	MIGR.	SIG LEVEL
Life-cycle characteristics						
Age	1979	t	–	43.50	37.28	.000*
Marital Status	1979	X2	–	insufficient cell size		
Family Size	1979	t	–	5.57	5.17	.001*
Children 0–4 years of age	1979	t	–	.67	.90	.000*
Nuclear families only	1042	t	–	.87	1.13	.000*
Place ties						
Previous Migration Experience	1979	X2	33.88	–	–	.000*
Duration of Residence (1)	1369	t	–	18.52	8.44	.000*
Kinship – number of						
same-surnamed persons	1979	t	–	19.39	12.38	.000*
same-surnamed heads	1979	t	–	3.73	2.43	.000*
Landownership	1979	X2	109.53	–	–	.000*
Economic condition						
Occupation	1979	X2	45.28	–	–	.000*
Economic Rank	1960	t	–	$423.44	$329.83	.000*
Value of Real Estate in 1860	1168	t	–	$2879.79	$1954.99	.000*
Other socio-demographics						
Race	1979	X2		insufficient cell size		
National Origin						
USA (1) / Foreign	1371	X2	27.66			.000*
German/Irish/British (2)/Other	156	X2		insufficient cell size		

* Significant at the .05 level.
1. Does not include natives of the town of enumeration in 1855.
2. English, Welsh, and Scottish.

than that of non-migrants.

Too few of the family heads were unmarried to test the importance of marital status, but family size was an important differential. Migrants headed significantly smaller families than non-migrants. Forty-seven percent of Schoharie's families were, however, augmented with employees or lodgers, extended with parents, siblings, or other relatives, or headed by unmarried individuals. In these families co-residents may have been superfluous to the decision to migrate. The number of children aged 0-4 years is, therefore, probably a better indicator of life-cycle stage. It was, moreover, an important differential. Out-migrants had a significantly greater number of children aged 0-4 than did non-migrants. This also was true of nuclear families alone. This suggests that migrants may have been seeking larger homes and environments with greater place utility in which to raise their presumably growing families.

Place ties

Each of the five indicators of place ties was a significant differential. These were previous migration experience, duration of residence by non-natives, two measures of kinship, and landownership.

The 560 natives of the town of enumeration, those
people who gave identical responses to the census
questions regarding age and duration of residence, were
significantly less likely to out-migrate than were
non-natives. Three of every ten (33.3 percent) of the
heads of families who had resided elsewhere were numbered
among the out-migrants. Only 17.5 percent of those
without prior migration experience were so counted.

Migrants were further differentiated from
non-migrants by duration of residence in their town of
residence in 1855. Among the 1,376 non-natives, the
average length of residence of migrants was 8.44 years,
ten years fewer than that of non-migrants. Moreover, 51.4
percent of those individuals resident less than five years
were migrants, compared with only 32 percent resident 5-9
years, 27.8 percent resident 10-14 years, and 14.8 percent
resident 15-19 years. Clearly, the lengthier one's
residence the less likely one was to out-migrate.

Kinship also was an important migration
differential. Heads of families who out-migrated had a
surname in common with twelve other residents, seven fewer
than the number shared by non-migrants. Each migrant was
also one of 2.43 family heads with the same last name.
Among non-migrants there were 3.73 related heads. Kinship
appears to have restricted out-migration.

Landownership was also a significant differential. Those who owned no land were more than twice as likely to out-migrate as those who were landowners (40.2 percent vs. 18.5 percent). People who owned property had invested in the community, an indication of a desire to be part of that community. Those who owned no land were relatively free to move on if they believed their opportunities to be better elsewhere. Conversely, landowners could not readily dispose of their assets. A poor crop year would also affect the neighbor who might otherwise be interested in acquiring one's farm if migration was contemplated. In a good crop year one might be less inclined to migrate than in poor years. Under these circumstances, landownership might be viewed as not only a constraint on migration but also a hindrance.

Economic factors

Economic factors were also important migration differentials. Occupation, economic rank, and the value of real estate owned in 1860 were found to be significant, but the value of personal estate in 1860 was not.

Male heads of families engaged in several dozen occupations in 1855. To analyze the effect of occupation on migration it was first necessary to collapse these into a small number of categories. Significant differences in migration behavior were found between those in the six resulting categories (Table 4.2). The 112 heads of families in the "upper class" were members of the most mobile groups. Those engaged in learned professions were twice as likely to migrate as farmers, the least mobile group.

Use of occupation as a migration differential in historical studies is problematic, however. Most social historians have been reluctant to establish more than four or five categories because the quality of the historical record, particularly the manuscript census, is questionable (Pessen, 1972). Sometimes this information was omitted, as it was for 6.4 percent of my sample. At other times one occupation was given for individuals who may have had several. Particularly common in this respect were farmers who probably earned the greater part of their annual income by hiring out as ice cutters, lumbermen, or shinglemakers during the winter months. Other people, for reasons that will never never be known, were apparently mislabled. Two examples from the Town of Gilboa are illustrative of how serious this problem can be. In 1855 Altron Maynard was enumerated as a farmer. In 1850 he had been a physician, an occupation he practiced (again?) in 1865. John Reed of Gilboa was also enumerated as a farmer in 1855. In the same year the credit ledgers of R. G. Dun and Company indicate that John Reed owned and operated

TABLE 4.2

OCCUPATION AND MOBILITY, 1855-1860 (1)
in percentages

Occupation	N	Non-Migrants	Migrants
Learned Professions	53	56.6	43.4
Businessmen, Clerks, and Civil Servants	118	64.4	35.6
Craftsmen	359	67.0	33.0
Farmers	1116	79.1	20.9
Laborers and Semi-skilled workers	197	70.4	29.6
No occupation reported	128	64.3	35.7

1 Occupational categories are found in Appendix F.

a general store and the two most important manufactories in Gilboa, a tannery and the Gilboa Cotton Textile Mill.

Michael Katz confronted this problem in two recent works. Rather than use occupation as the sole measure of socio-economic status in his 1975 study of Hamilton, he combined it with property assessment information for each household. Similarly, in a 1978 study of length of residence in Erie County, New York, per family dwelling value was calculated from the 1855 census data (Katz et al., 1978). Assuming that high-status people resided in high-valued homes and, conversely, that lesser-status people resided in lesser-valued homes; it was concluded that the resultant value is "a rough proxy for economic rank" (p. 691).

I used this same measure of socio-economic status and found that migrants from Schoharie were of lesser status than non-migrants. The average dwelling value for out-migrants was $329.83, almost $100 less than that of houses occupied by non-migrants. This suggests that non-migrants had greater incomes than out-migrants.

Economic differentials between non-migrants and out-migrants found in the 1860 census were also assssed in terms of the value of real estate and value of personal property reported in the census of 1860. The value of real estate was significantly greater for non-migrants than out-migrants but that of personal property was not.

It appears that those who persisted were considerably better off than those who had migrated, but it cannot be determined whether or not out-migrants changed their economic condition at rates different from those of non-migrants. However, neither of these variables is a differential in the proper sense because they are not pre-migration attributes.

Farmers

Analysis of farm size, value, and production, as reported in the agricultural schedules of the 1855 census, provides a more complete picture of the factors affecting the decision to migrate made by farmers. Non-migrant farmers seem to have owned and operated significantly larger, more valuable, and more productive farms than those operated by out-migrant farmers (Table 4.3). Moreover, every measure of life-cycle characteristics, place ties, economic rank, and national origin was also a significant differential. Non-migrant farmers were likely to be older, a town native or long-time resident, members of large kinship networks, and landowmers. They also resided in higher valued dwellings, and if not town natives, were more likely to be American-born than foreign-born.

TABLE 4.3

BIVARIATE ANALYSES OF NON-MIGRANT AND OUT-MIGRANT FARMERS

CHARACTERISTIC	N	TEST	X2	MEANS NON-MIGR.	MEANS MIGR.	SIG LEVEL
Life-cycle characteristics						
Age	1116	t	–	44.93	38.03	.000*
Family Size	1116	t	–	5.70	5.22	.003*
Children 0-4 years of age	1116	t	–	.63	.88	.000*
Nuclear families only	547	t	–	.79	1.11	.001*
Place ties						
Previous Migration Experience	1112	X2	15.92	–	–	.000*
Duration of Residence (1)	710	t	–	21.64	10.19	.000*
Kinship – same-surnamed persons	1116	t	–	22.40	14.76	.000*
– same-surnamed heads	1116	t	–	4.29	2.92	.000*
Landownership	1116	X2	46.52	–	–	.000*
Economic condition						
Economic Rank	1099	t	–	$395.87	$243.32	.000*
Other socio-demographics						
Nativity: USA (1) / Foreign	710	X2	12.48	–	–	.000*
Agricultural characteristics						
Improved acreage	1116	t	–	64.48	42.99	.000*
Unimproved acreage	1116	t	–	32.73	20.99	.000*
Total acreage	1116	t	–	97.23	63.99	.000*
Percentage improved acreage	1116	t	–	57.60	44.91	.000*
Value of farmland	1108	t	–	$2631.02	$1422.18	.000*
Value of livestock	1116	t	–	$ 432.03	$ 264.99	.000*
Value of agricultural implements	1116	t	–	$ 124.22	$ 67.75	.000*
Total value	1108	t	–	$3163.43	$1754.92	.000*
Value per acre of farmland	1108	t	–	$ 27.78	$ 19.91	.014*

* Significant at the .05 level.
1. Does not include natives of the town of enumeration in 1855.

The value of real estate and the value of personal property as reported in the census manuscripts of 1860 were significant differentials between non-migrant and out-migrant farmers who owned land in 1855 and were found in the 1860 census manuscripts (Table 4.4). The value of real estate in 1860 of non-migrant farmers was more than one and one-half times greater than that owned by out-migrants farmers. The value of personal property of non-migrant farmers was one-third again as great as that of out-migrant farmers. Although these variables, as noted above, should not be considered migration differentials, it seems clear that non-migrants were more prosperous than out-migrants.

Land availability may have been an important factor affecting the decision to migrate among farmers. Population density in Schoharie County was high (56 people per square mile) and the best farmland had been cultivated for two or more generations. Recent in-migrants and newly formed households may have been compelled to take up farming on the less productive upland soils of the county. Moreover, given the rapid commercialization and increasing specialization of agriculture in the county, they may not have been able to compete with established farmers. Out-migration was a viable alternative for those who wished to do more than subsist.

TABLE 4.4

MOBILITY AND WEALTH
IN 1860 OF FARMERS WITH LAND IN 1855

	N	Non-Migrants	Migrants	Sig Level
Real Estate	734	$3498.52	$2426.84	.000*
Personal	701	$1164.11	$ 813.32	.004*

* significant at the .05 level.

Other socio-demographic factors

Race was expected to influence migration, but no significant difference between whites and non-whites was found. Schoharie´s 46 blacks and mulattos were slightly more likely to persist than whites, a suggestion that that rural non-whites may not have suffered from the same kinds of discrimination experienced by non-whites in urban areas. Rural non-whites were, however, no less likely to occupy the lowest rung on the socio-economic ladder than their urban counterparts. The overwhelming majority of those in Schoharie were landless farmers and unskilled laborers who resided in the least valued housing. Most were descendents of slaves brought to Schoharie by Dutch settlers in the mid-1700s, but their deep roots in the county did not make them less subject to segregation than urban blacks or rural blacks in the South. Those in the Town of Schoharie resided in either the area between Foxes Creek and the Old Stone Fort, about two miles north of the Court House, or in the marshy area in the village of Schoharie between the Court House and the old Lutheran Parsonage.

National origin was also an important migration differential. Among those born outside the town of enumeration the American-born were significantly less likely to leave than were the foreign-born (Table 4.5).

TABLE 4.5

MOBILITY AND NATIONAL ORIGIN

	N	Non-Migrants	Migrants
USA born (1)	1215	72.2	27.8
Foreign born	156	51.3	48.7

1 Excludes the 560 natives of the town
  of enumeration.

There were no differences in behavior within these two groups. Those born in Schoharie County were no less likely to migrate than those born elsewhere in New York or in a state other than New York. The Irish, Germans, British, and other undifferentiated foreign-born were also represented equally among migrants and non-migrants.

Migration: Multivariate Analysis of the Sample

Thus far, it has been shown using bivariate techniques that several explanatory variables are important migration differentials. The relative strength of each of these is yet to be determined. Moreover, these explanatory variables may not be independent. For example, Thernstrom and Knights (1971:33-34) found that national origin and occupation are correlated because immigrants usually are employed in lower-status jobs. This correlation means that the estimated effect of occupation on migration would be inflated above its "true" effect after considering the effect of national origin. Other complex interrelationships between explanatory variables probably exist and need to be uncovered. Landownership, for example, may be affected by age, duration of residence, and occupation.

Several multivariate techniques that estimate the true effects of each explanatory variable while controlling for correlations with all other variables are available. A limited number are appropriate when the dependent variable is dichotomous. Multiple Classification Analysis, "the ´technique of choice´ for most problems in quantitative social history" is one such technique (Jensen, 1978). Examples of its use may be found in Laslett (1977) and Katz, Doucet, and Stern (1978). MCA, an analysis of variance-based technique is available in the Statistical Package for the Social Sciences (Nie et al., 1975:409-410). The MCA version in SPSS is, however, limited in the number of explanatory factors (categorical independent variables) and covariates (interval scale variables) permitted. It will accept a maximum of five of each. Moreover, the SPSS version of MCA does not test for covariate-by-factor interaction. It is not possible then to test for correlation between landownership, a categorical variable, and age, an interval scale variable, without first categorizing age and using it as a factor in a non-covariate design.

Multiple Classification Analysis was undertaken by first selecting five variables that collectively might best explain behavior of the sample. At least one from each of the four major groups of differentials was chosen. Those selected were chosen because the existing literature and the bivariate analyses presented above suggested them to be the most important differentials. These included: 1) age in 1855 categorized into nine five-year cohorts, 2) whether or not the person owned land, 3) the numer of same surnamed heads of families resident in the town of enumeration, 4) a variable that combined national origin and duration of residence, and 5) economic rank measured by per family dwelling value in quintiles.

The five variables explained only 16.5 percent of the variation in migration behavior. Column 1 of the MCA Table (Table 4.6) gives the the variable label and the categories of each. Column 2 gives the number of cases in each category. Column 3 gives the deviation of the values in each category assumming a mean of zero. A positive value indicates a category in which cases are more likely than not to have migrated. Moreover, these values indicate the relative strength of each category of each variable. A case falling in a category with a value of .10 is more likely to migrate than is one falling in a category with a value of .05. Column 4 is the Eta value, a bivariate beta for the variable being evaluated. Column 5 gives the deviation for each category of each variable (as in column 3) but controls for correlations between variables. The smaller differences between the extremes of categories for each variable indicate that the explanatory variables are not independent; the effect of

TABLE 4.6
MCA OF MOBILITY WITH OCCUPATION

Variable + Category	N	Unadjusted DEV"N	ETA	Adjusted DEV"N	BETA
Age by five year cohort					
1 Less than 25	88	.12		.10	
2 25 to 29	261	.11		.07	
3 30 to 34	318	.09		.06	
4 35 to 39	299	.03		-.01	
5 40 to 44	256	.02		.02	
6 45 to 49	199	-.07		-.04	
7 50 to 54	184	-.11		-.07	
8 55 to 59	111	-.12		-.06	
9 60 or more	228	-.16		-.09	
			.22		.14
Landownership					
0 Does not own land	714	.13		.08	
1 Owns land	1230	-.08		-.05	
			.23		.14
Same-surnamed heads					
1 One	726	.11		.05	
2 Two	374	-.00		.00	
3 3 4 5	482	-.09		-.06	
4 6 or more	362	-.09		-.02	
			.20		.11
Nativity and residence					
1 Native of town	587	-.09		-.07	
2 USA, Rez < 5 Y	363	.23		.18	
3 USA, Rez 5-9 Y	158	-.00		-.03	
4 USA, Rez 10-14 Y	117	.01		.00	
5 USA, Rez 15+ Y	564	-.12		-.07	
6 Non-US, Rez < 5 Y	71	.30		.19	
7 Non-US, Rez 5-9 Y	45	.27		.17	
8 Non-US, Rez 10-14 Y	16	.05		-.03	
9 Non-US, Rez 15+ Y	23	-.00		.01	
			.34		.24
Occupational Category					
1 Learned Professions	48	.20		.11	
2 Business and Civil	107	.09		.03	
3 Craftsmen	356	.07		.02	
4 Farmers	1110	-.06		-.00	
5 Laborers etc	197	.03		-.07	
6 No occupation report	126	.09		-.01	
			.15		.07

Multiple R Squared   .165
Multiple R   .406
Grand Mean =   1.26

each variable considered separately is greater than the effect of the variable after controlling for the effects of all other variables.

It is of considerable interest that, overall, the relationships extant for the categories of each variable did not change from columns 3 to 5. Only one variable was not consistent in this respect. The unadjusted deviation (col 3) for same-surnamed heads suggests that members of increasingly larger kinship networks exhibited an increasingly greater tendency toward persistence. The adjusted deviation (col 5) suggests that members of the largest kin groups are actually more likely to migrate than are members of medium sized kinship networks. Individuals without kin nevertheless were more likely to out-migrate than were those who had nearby relatives.

It is also clear that individuals resident less than five years were considerably more likely to out-migrate than were those resident a greater number of years. This is the most important migration differential. Moreover, among those resident five or more years, the American-born were more likely to persist than the foreign-born. This suggests that at mid-nineteenth century older rural areas of the United States had less difficulty absorbing fellow Americans into the mainstream of community life than it did foreigners. For example, residents with cultural backgrounds not common to

Schoharie may have been inclined to out-migrate and seek people of like heritage. Irish and German Catholics may have left because they could not support establishment of a Roman Catholic Church in the county. Other foreigners may likewise have been uncomfortable in what was largely a Protestant, Anglo-German community.

Column 6 gives the partial beta for each variable. Because the explanatory variables are not independent of each other these are lower than the Eta values in column 4. These Beta coefficients are analagous to those in a multiple regression analysis and are, therefore, proportional to the explanatory power of each independent variable. Nativity and duration of residence is the strongest of the five variables in the model. Landownership and age are of comparable strength in predicting migration behavior. Occupation is the least important.

A second MCA that substituted occupation in 1855 for economic rank produced nearly identical results (Table 4.7). The R squared in both models was .165. The affect of age was the same and that of landownership, kinship, and national origin/duration of residence insignificantly different. Occupation was a slightly better indicator of migration than economic rank, but since the occupational categories were established using subjective criteria, greater confidence is placed in the

TABLE 4.7
MCA OF MOBILITY WITH ECONOMIC RANK

Variable + Category	N	Unadjusted DEV"N	ETA	Adjusted DEV"N	BETA
Age by five year cohort					
1 Less than 25	86	.12		.09	
2 25 to 29	258	.11		.07	
3 30 to 34	308	.09		.06	
4 35 to 39	294	.03		-.00	
5 40 to 44	251	.02		.02	
6 45 to 49	195	-.07		-.04	
7 50 to 54	184	-.11		-.08	
8 55 to 59	109	-.12		-.06	
9 60 or greater	226	-.16		-.09	
			.22		.14
Landownership					
0 Does not own land	696	.14		.07	
1 Owns land	1215	-.08		-.04	
			.24		.12
Same-surnamed heads					
1 One	707	.11		.06	
2 Two	369	-.00		-.00	
3 3 4 5	477	-.09		-.07	
4 6 or more	358	-.09		-.02	
			.21		.12
Nativity and residence					
1 Native of town	576	-.09		-.07	
2 US, Rez <5 Years	357	.23		.18	
3 US, Rez 5-9 Y	157	-.01		-.03	
4 US, Rez 10-14 Y	116	.01		.00	
5 US, Rez 15+ Years	554	-.12		-.06	
6 Non-US, Rez <5 Y	69	.30		.17	
7 Non-US, Rez 5-9 Y	44	.28		.16	
8 Non-US, Rez 10-14 Y	15	.07		-.01	
9 Non-US, Rez 15+ Y	23	-.00		.01	
			.34		.23
Economic Rank					
1 Lowest Quintile	394	.08		.02	
2 Second Quintile	373	.06		.03	
3 Middle Quintile	382	-.00		.01	
4 Fourth Quintile	317	-.07		-.04	
5 Highest Quintile	445	-.07		-.02	
			.14		.05

Multiple R Squared   .165
Multiple R   .406
Grand Mean =   1.26

results of the MCA that incorporated economic rank. The apparent close positive correlation between occupational category (assumming an ordinal classification of groups 1 through 5) and economic rank seems to validate use of occupation as a surrogate for socio-economic status in studies of the nineteenth century.

Landowning farmers

The migration behavior of farmers who owned land was explored with MCA using variables from both the population and the agricultural schedules of the 1855 census. Selected from the former was one variable representative of each of the major groups of differentials. These were age, same-surnamed heads, and national origin/duration of residence. Because all of the variables from the agricultural schedule were significant in bivariate analyses, I selected the two that probably best exemplified the economic prospects of any given farm. These were: 1) total acreage, and 2) dollar value per acre. The 20.5 percent of farmers who did not own land were excluded from this analysis because data for them was not provided in the agricultural schedule. These individuals may have been farm laborers who were mislabeled.

Although only 15 percent of the variance in migration behavior was explained, it generally appears to be true that landowning farmers who migrated were young, recent in-migrants to Schoharie (Table 4.8). Individuals resident in Schoharie less than five years were significantly more likely to leave than were those resident longer. This may have varied between American-born and foreign-born, but the number of the latter is too small to render a conclusion. Kinship had the same effect upon landowning farmers as it did upon the entire population. Those least likely to leave were members of small kinship groups. Those without kin were more likely to out-migrate than others.

The second most important findings are those related to the agricultural variables. Farmers for whom no data were reported in the agricultural census were more likely to out-migrate than those who had "real" farms. Farmers who owned land but who had no farm probably owned their house and lot house and lot and little, if anything, else. They were undoubtedly only marginally better off than landless farmers. Farmers with sizeable acreages or high valued property were significantly more likely to remain than were those with smaller or lesser valued properties. This may have been related to the location of these farms. Those in the "Schoharie Flats" were in rich alluvial material and may have been small, high valued

TABLE 4.8
MCA OF MOBILITY BY LANDOWNING FARMERS

Variable + Category	N	Unadjusted DEV"N	ETA	Adjusted DEV"N	BETA
Age by five year cohort					
1 Less than 25 Y	26	.30		.21	
2 25 to 29	90	.11		.09	
3 30 to 34	129	.08		.06	
4 35 to 39	105	.05		.04	
5 40 to 44	113	-.02		-.01	
6 45 to 49	107	-.04		-.01	
7 50 to 54	104	-.07		-.06	
8 55 to 59	69	-.09		-.06	
9 60 or more	141	-.10		-.09	
			.24		.18
Same-surnamed heads					
1 One	226	.08		.04	
2 Two	179	.03		.02	
3 3 4 5	253	-.06		-.06	
4 6 or more	226	-.03		.00	
			.15		.10
Nativity and residence					
1 Native of town	329	-.05		-.05	
2 USA, Rez <5 Years	117	.27		.21	
3 USA, Rez 5-9 Years	38	.02		.01	
4 USA, Rez 10-14 Y	50	.01		-.01	
5 USA, Rez 15+ Years	326	-.06		-.03	
6 Non-US, Rez <5 Years	6	.17		.07	
7 Non-US, Rez 5-9 Y	4	.08		.04	
8 Non-US, Rez 10-14 Y	2	.33		.26	
9 Non-US, Rez 15+ Y	12	.08		.10	
			.30		.23
Total farm acreage					
1 None recorded	85	.16		.20	
2 .5 to 63.5 acres	186	.04		.03	
3 64 to 99 acres	167	-.02		-.05	
4 100 to 145 acres	239	-.00		-.01	
5 146 or more acres	207	-.08		-.06	
			.18		.19
Value per acre					
1 No value given	86	.16		-.09	
2 .25 to $15.99	191	.01		.03	
3 $16 to $25.00	204	-.01		.03	
4 $25.01 to $37.40	199	-.04		-.02	
5 $37.41 to highest	204	-.03		-.00	
			.15		.10

Multiple R Squared   .151
Multiple R   .388
Grand Mean = 1.17

plots. Farms on hillsides or ridges may have made up in acreage what they lacked in soil quality. The least prosperous farms were those that were small in acreage and located on the rocky uplands of the county (Conklin, 1974: Ellis, 1946). Those who farmed the latter lands were undoubtedly those who found it most difficult to make the transition from cash grain production to dairying. They certainly would have lacked the requisite capital to do so. If they were also young and without investments in Schoharie other than the land they farmed it seems likely that they may have sold out to their more prosperous, established neighbors and sought their fortunes elsewhere.

Summary

The socio-demographic and economic characteristics of potential migrants were of some importance in explaining the migration behavior of heads of families in a typical rural area of New York during the mid-1800s. Bi-variate analyses indicate that several were significant differentials but multivariate analysis demonstrates that collectively these differentials were not as important in predicting the behavior as one is led to expect given the findings of other researchers. The process of migration selectivity in rural areas of New York in the mid 1800s seems to have been a highly complex process not fully explained by the variables analyzed in this study.

Three possible differentials not examined are suggested. First, position in a kinship network was probably correlated with the likelihood of acquiring property through inheritance. Heads of families who stood to gain little, if any, real estate upon the death of an elder kin may have been more inclined to out-migrate than heads who stood to inherit sizable acreages. Similarly, landless farm families who operated farms owned by kin were probably less likely to out-migrate than were landless tenants. Second, the Panic of 1857 briefly depressed business and recently hired laborers, craftsmen, and clerks may have been the first employees fired. If this were the case, recent in-migrants to the county, many of whom were Irish and German immigrants, would have born the brunt of these dismissals. Third, death of a family member may have produced traumas that were overcome only by departure from the place associated with the deceased. The extent to which these and other variables affected the decision to migrate should be explored.

It appears that the socio-demographic and economic differentials identified in this study are consistent with those found by other scholars. The "typical" head of an out-migrant family was a recent in-migrant without relatives in the study area, relatively young, and landless. He was also likely to be of lesser economic rank than non-migrant heads of families, an indication that he had not achieved the same level of "success" in his field of endeavor that his "co-workers" had. If he was a landowning farmer, he was also likely to be without a farm or the possessor of one with marginal potential. In general, it appears that the socio-demographic and economic characteristics of heads of families were important indicators of a family's likely migration behavior. Duration of residence was consistently the most important of these characteristics.

Notes

1. My data suggest that during the mid-nineteenth century single-member households consisting of an elderly person were exceedingly rare. Most elderly widows and widowers lived with daughters. Elderly couples were more likely to reside with sons.

2. The size of some kinship networks was probably underestimated because town boundaries bisect their distribution. Moreover, maternal relatives who do not share the paternal surname are not counted. In the absence of complete genealogical records the method adopted is the most pragmatic possible.

CHAPTER 5

DESTINATIONS AND DIFFERENTIALS

Existing studies of migration within the United States during the nineteenth century seem to imply that urban centers and the western frontier were the foremost destinations of rural out-migrants (see Chapter 2). Although the behavior of out-migrants from a specific rural locale has not been investigated, the following explanations of in-migration patterns have been offered. Farmers on the eastern seaboard abandoned the overworked soils of that region for the virgin soils of the West or nearby manufacturing centers. People engaging in non-farm activities in rural areas of the East experienced a decline in their personal prosperity as farmers left and these non-farmers availed themselves of opportunities presented by emergent urban centers of the frontier and older, established commercial and manufacturing centers of the East. The possibility that most rural out-migrants did not participate in a westward or urbanward movement has not been addressed.

Differentials among out-migrants from a given locale differentiated by distance migrated have not been examined either. Short-distance migration is, for example, closely associated with life-cycle. Movement to nearby places is often a response to changes in family size and ages of off-spring. Longer distance migration is more closely associated with employment. (Rose, 1958). Higher status/skilled jobs are fewer in number in proportion to the total number of employment opportunities and are concentrated in fewer places. Individuals engaged in these occupations generally migrate greater distances to secure employment than do those engaged in more uniformly distributed lesser status/skilled jobs (Glasco, 1978; Modell, 1971; Rose, 1958).

The socio-demographic and economic characteristics of urbanward migrants also may differ from those of long distance migrants with rural destinations but the existing literature has not addressed this issue. Were age, family size, and other life-cycle characteristics correlated with the type of environment to which rural out-migrants went? Did landownership, kinship, and other place ties have a bearing on the choice of destination type? To what extent was occupation associated with one or the other of these two destinations? These and related questions must be addressed if one is to gain a fuller understanding of migration selectivity within nineteenth century America.

This chapter focuses on three aspects of rural out-migration during the mid-1800s. The expected and observed destinations of out-migrants from the study area are examined in the first. The socio-demographic and economic differentials between short distance migrants and longer distance migrants are analyzed in the second. Differentials between urbanward migrants and migrants to rural places are investigated in the third.

Models of Out-Migration

The gravity model suggests that the volume of migration to and from any given place often is related to the distance between a given pair of origins and destinations plus some "weight" that expresses the probable interaction between this pair of places (Lee, 1966; Ravenstein, 1876, 1885, 1889). The weight most commonly associated with these places is population size (Carrothers, 1956; Zipf, 1946). Since the employment opportunities, social contacts, etc. in a place are closely related to its size, the number of inhabitants is often an appropriate measure of place attractiveness.

Two modifications of the basic gravity model also have been effective in modeling migration behavior. The first of these is based upon "intervening opportunities" (Stouffer, 1940; 1960). Stouffer asserts that the volume of migration between a given pair of origins and destinations is related to the number of alternative destinations between this pair, and not the linear distance between them. In this sense, the intended destination is competing with every place along the migrant's route of travel. The probability that the migrant will find a satisfactory alternative to his intended destination is associated with the number of places encountered and evaluated.

The second modification of the gravity model incorporates "migrant stock", the number of people of a given origin resident at a given destination, as an alternative to population size (Greenwood, 1969; Nelson, 1959). According to Mangalam (1968:17) "migrants seek a destination where their deprivations or unmet wants can be satisfied" and "go to a place where the social organization is as closely related as possible (in their perception) to the one in their place of origin." Thus, migration is likely to be channelized between distant places of like social environments despite the existence of closer, economically satisfactory places. The whereabouts of previous migrants from a given place are, therefore, probable indicators of socially similar environments and likely destinations of potential migrants (Dunlevy and Gemeny, 1977; McInnis, 1969).

The underlying rationale for these migration models is an assumption regarding the process of gathering information undertaken by potential migrants. The amount and kind of data one is likely to possess about any given place is closely associated with two factors: proximity and type of contact. An individual should know more about those places immediately surrounding his place of residence than about those places more distant. These nearby places are those through which he may travel while en route to work, to shop, etc., or about which he knows from other personal experience or through various local media. Information about more distant places also may be gathered from personal experience such as vacation travel or previous residence, but interpersonal communication with friends and relatives who already migrated is a more important source of data about distant places (Erickson, 1972; Hagerstrand, 1947; Hudson, 1973; Rice and Ostergren, 1978).

Partial and Total Displacement Migrants

The processes presented above act in concert to produce two types of migrants. These are short distance, or partial displacement, migrants and longer-distance, or total displacement, migrants (Roseman, 1969). Short-distance migrants should be the more numerous of the two types of migrants (Ravenstein, 1885). Partial displacement migrants change their place of residence but retain some elements of their former activity spaces including places of business, socialization, and employment. Total displacement migration is associated with change in every aspect of an individual's activity

space and, hence, involves relocation over longer
distances.

Studies by Hagerstrand (1947), Langholm (1975),
and Miller (1973) document the relative importance of
short-distance migration during the nineteenth century and
tend to confirm the general applicability of the gravity
model in explaining migration patterns. Hagerstrand
(1947) found that 485, or 76.9 percent, of the 631
migratory movements to the parish of Asby, Ostergotland,
Sweden, in the period 1860-69, originated no more than
17km distant. Moreover, "about one-third of all movements
between dwellings escape out figures when we define
migration as movements between parishes" (1962:70). He
concluded (1962:70) that roughly 83 percent of all
domicile changes appear to have taken place within a
radius of about 10 miles. Similarly, Langholm (1975),
using place of birth data in the Norwegian Population
Census of 1865, found that 52.1 percent of the
non-institutional in-migrants to the commune of Ullensaker
were born in neighboring communes no more than 17km
distant. Because these data reflect the sum of movements
prior to the census and not, as Hagerstrand's do, every
movement within a given time period, Langholm concluded
(p. 39) that "the relative importance of short-distance
migration very well may be the same in the two areas
studied" (p. 39). Miller (1973) examined in-migration to

Syracuse, New York, and found that 41 percent of the
people who arrived in the city between 1850 and 1855 were
intra-county migrants who had traveled no more than 20
miles. Only 8.6 percent of the city's recent in-migrants
could be traced to previous places of residence outside
Onondaga County.

Rural and Urban Migrants

Rural out-migrants may also be differentiated on
the basis of rural and urban destination types. The
former consists of individuals who migrate to nearby or
more distant places environmentally similar to that of
their place of origin. The latter consists of individuals
who are attracted to urban places or to rural places
adjacent to cities by a number of factors including
employment opportunities, social contacts, and alternative
lifestyles. Some urbanward migrants move directly into
the city. Others move to locations on the periphery of
cities where something resembling a rural environment may
still exist. A third type of urbanward migrant moves
stepwise, or in stages, from farm to village, and then
village to city. All of these are urbanward in the sense
that they are either environmentally or spatially closer
to urban places than they were before (Conway, 1980;
Ravenstein, 1876, 1885, 1889; Redford, 1926).

Out-Migration Fields

Partial displacement migration and total displacement migration are both evident in the observed pattern of out-migration from the study area (Figs. 5.1 through 5.6). Most of the out-migrant families found in 1860 or 1865 moved relatively short-distances (Table 5.1). Sixty-one percent of these, and 39 percent of the 522 known or assumed out-migrant families, went to towns contiguous to those in which they resided in 1855. These family groups moved an average distance of seven miles, based upon the straight line distance between town centers. An additional 59 families, 12.6 percent of those found, settled in towns bordering those contiguous to their town of residence in 1855. The average distance migrated by these families was 13.36 miles. These two groups of short-distance migrants constitute 77 percent of the 364 migrant families found, or 50.7 percent of all known or assummed out-migrants. The average distance migrated by these 265 families was 8.09 miles.

Although a majority of the out-migrants moved relatively short-distances the proportion of partial displacement migrants appears to be much less than one might expect given the studies by Hagerstrand (1947), Langholm (1975), and Miller (1973). This conclusion should not be drawn. This study defined migration on the

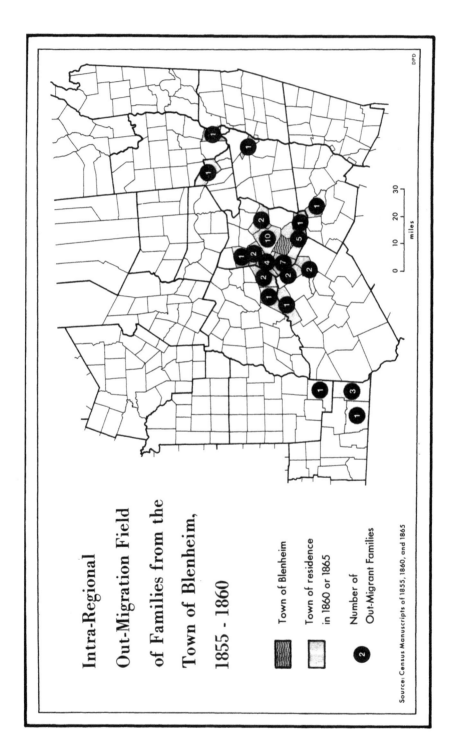

Intra-Regional
Out-Migration Field
of Families from the
Town of Blenheim,
1855 - 1860

Town of Blenheim

Town of residence
in 1860 or 1865

Number of
Out-Migrant Families

2

Source: Census Manuscripts of 1855, 1860, and 1865

Figure 5.1

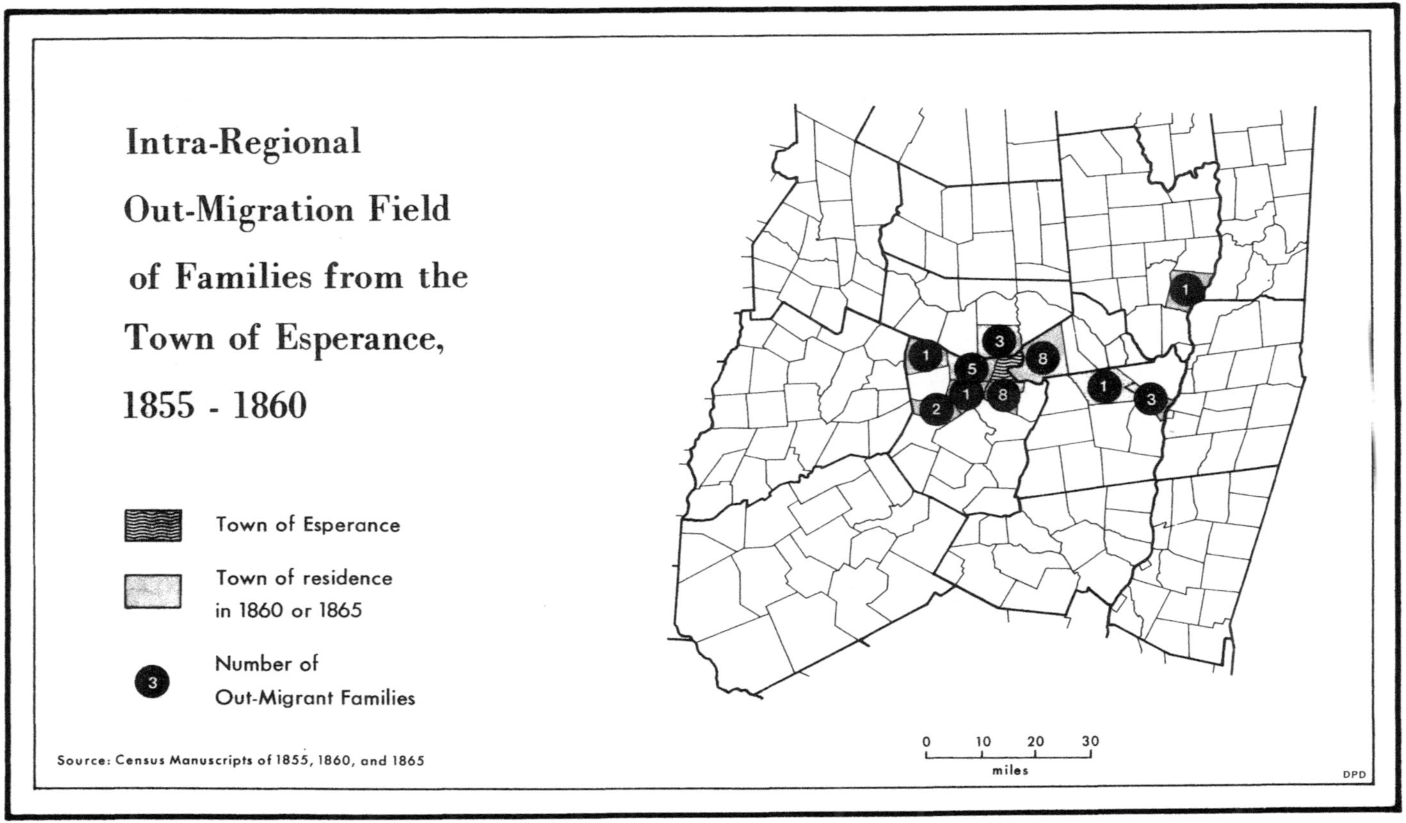

Intra-Regional
Out-Migration Field
of Families from the
Town of Esperance,
1855 - 1860

Town of Esperance

Town of residence
in 1860 or 1865

Number of
Out-Migrant Families

3

Source: Census Manuscripts of 1855, 1860, and 1865

miles

0   10   20   30

Figure 5.2

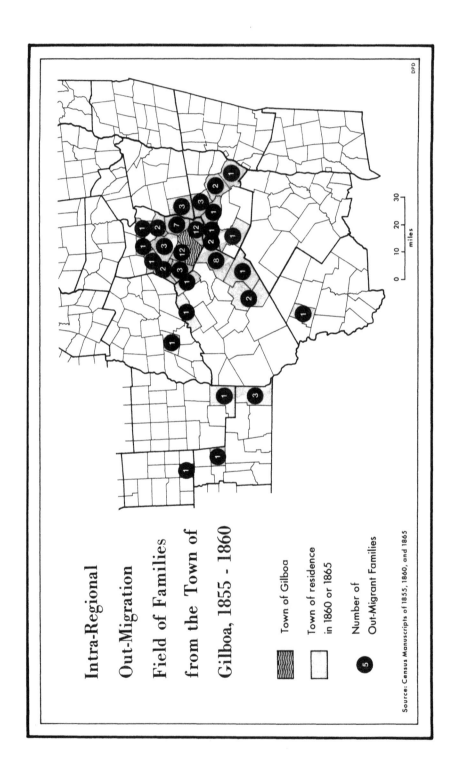

Intra-Regional
Out-Migration
Field of Families
from the Town of
Gilboa, 1855 - 1860

Town of Gilboa

Town of residence
in 1860 or 1865

Number of
Out-Migrant Families

5

Source: Census Manuscripts of 1855, 1860, and 1865

Figure 5.3

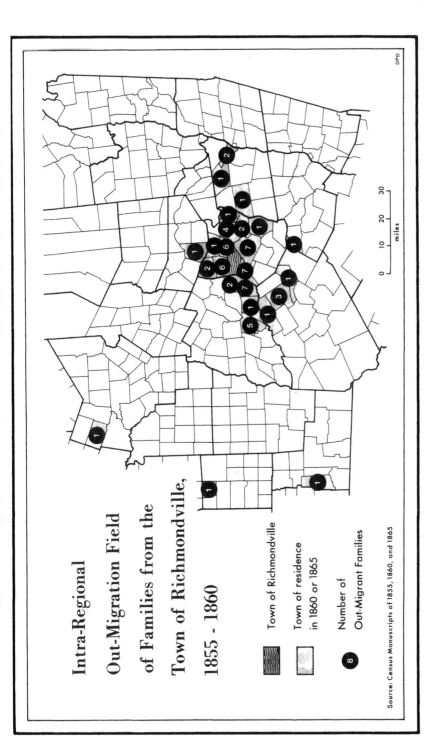

Intra-Regional Out-Migration Field of Families from the Town of Richmondville, 1855 - 1860

Town of Richmondville

Town of residence in 1860 or 1865

Number of Out-Migrant Families

8

Source: Census Manuscripts of 1855, 1860, and 1865

0   10   20   30
miles

DPD

Figure 5.4

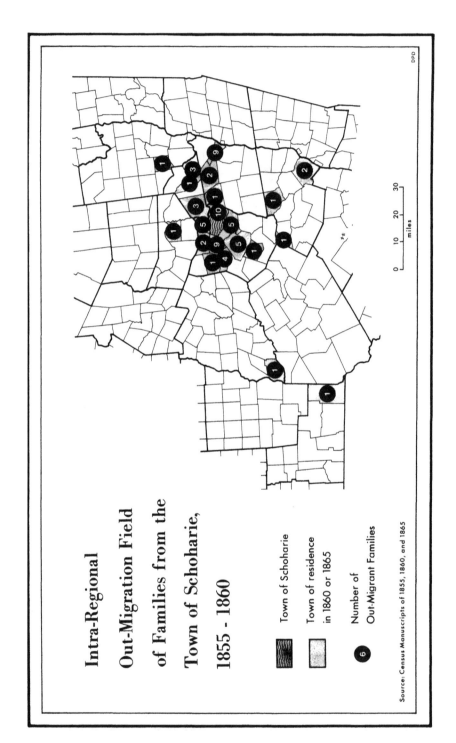

Intra-Regional
Out-Migration Field
of Families from the
Town of Schoharie,
1855 - 1860

Town of Schoharie

Town of residence
in 1860 or 1865

Number of
Out-Migrant Families

6

Source: Census Manuscripts of 1855, 1860, and 1865

DPD

miles

0   10   20   30

Figure 5.5

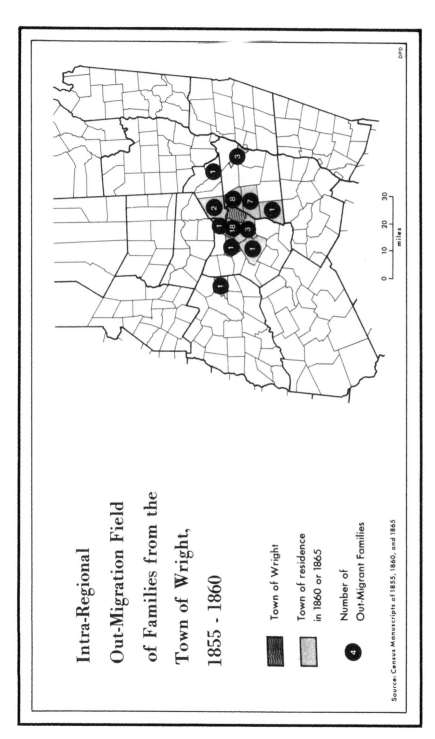

Intra-Regional
Out-Migration Field
of Families from the
Town of Wright,
1855 - 1860

Town of Wright

Town of residence
in 1860 or 1865

Number of
Out-Migrant Families

4

Source: Census Manuscripts of 1855, 1860, and 1865

miles

0   10   20   30

DPD

Figure 5.6

TABLE 5.1

DESTINATIONS OF 522 OUT-MIGRANT FAMILIES

Partial Displacement Migrants		206
(Contiguous Towns)		
Transitional Families		59
(Towns bordering contiguous towns)		
Total Displacement Migrants		257
Places within New York State		
Rural	43	
Urban	31	
Total	74	
Places outside New York		
Rural	15	
Urban	10	
Total	25	
Unknown Destinations	158	
Grand Total		522

basis of detected inter-town movement; an unknown, but possibly large, number of people who changed dwellings within the sample towns were not included in the sample population of out-migrants. Hence the results presented here understate partial displacement migration and overstate the average distance moved by partial displacement migrants.

Clear differentiation between partial displacement migrants and total displacement migrants is also problematic. The 59 families who moved to towns bordering contiguous towns may or may not have been partial displacement migrants. Some may have continued to attend church and to regularly conduct business with merchants in their previous places of residence. Others should be classified as total displacement migrants because they formed new associations. Unfortunately, neither the historical literature nor contemporary studies of the 1850s document the geographic extent of rural activity spaces. However, it should be obvious that modes of transportation would be the primary constraint given that a ten mile trip by farm wagon to the nearest grist mill was a full days journey made infrequently (Conklin, 1974:50). These 59 families who moved into a zone of transition are not easily classified. They will be excluded from subsequent analyses of differentials between partial displacement migrants and total displacement migrants.

Return migration appears to have been an important factor in the pattern of partial displacement migration. Selected out-migrant families who reported their duration of residence as less than five years were sought in the 1850 census to determine their place of residence in that year. Using the index to heads of households in the 1850 census proved expedient; 58 of the 148 located in either 1860 or 1865 were recaptured.(1) Thirty-six who probably headed households in 1850 and fifty-four who probably did not could not be traced using the index as a finding aid. Thirty-seven percent (14 of 38) of those who moved from their 1855 town of residence to an adjacent town returned to their town of residence in 1850. Only 10 percent (2 of 20) of those who moved to non-contiguous towns were return migrants.

Fewer than half of the 522 families were longer-distance or total displacement migrants. Moreover, the destinations of the 99 such families located in 1860 were rather dispersed throughout east-central New York and four states of the Upper Mississippi River Valley (Table 5.2). Evidence of channelized migration exists for only four destinations, three within New York state. All five of the families that went to the Village of Portlandville (Town of Milford, Otsego County) were from

TABLE 5.2

PLACES OF RESIDENCE IN 1860 OF
106 TOTALLY DISPLACED MIGRANT FAMILIES

State County: City or Town	Out-Migrant Families from the Town of						
	1	2	3	4	5	6	T
New York							
Albany: Albany	1	3		2	9	3	18
: Berne					1		1
: Guilderland		1		1	2		4
Broome: Barker			1				1
: Colesville	1						1
: Stanford	3		3		1		7
: Union				1			1
: Windsor	1						1
Chenango: Afton	1	1					2
Cortland: Marathon			1				1
: Preble				1			1
Delaware: Andes		2					2
: Davenport	1	1	1				3
: Kortright			3				3
: Stamford			1				1
Greene: Cairo		2					2
: Catskill		1		2			3
: Durham				1			1
: Prattsville				1	1		2
: Windham	1						1
Montgomery: Glen					1		1
: Root				1			1
Oneida: Camden				1			1
Otsego: Laurens			1				1
: Maryland	1						1
: Milford				5			5
: Roseboom						1	1
: Unadilla					1		1
Saratoga: Ballston Spa					1		1
: Half Moon	1						1
: Stillwater		1					1
Schenectady: Glenville	1						1
: Schenectady					3	1	4
: Rotterdam					1		1
Schoharie: Blenheim					1		1
: Cobleskill			1				1
: Richmondville			1				1
: Schoharie			1				1
: Seward	1						1
: Wright			1				1
Sullivan: Callicoon			1				1

TABLE 5.2 (cont.)

State County: City or Town	Out-Migrant Families from the Town of						
	1	2	3	4	5	6	T
Illinois							
Cook: Leyden Center					1		1
Jo Daviess: Hanover		1					1
Kankakee: Kankakee					1		1
LaSalle: Mendota				2			2
Logan: Lincoln						7	7
McHenry: Chemung	1						1
Iowa							
Delaware: South Fork				1			1
Minnesota							
Steele: Summit			1				1
Pennsylvania							
Westchester					1		1
Wisconsin							
Fond du Lac: Ripon			1				1
LaCrosse: Barre			1				1
Monroe: Portland					1		1
Racine: Raymond	1						1
Rock: Harmony					1		1
Walworth: Darien		1					1
: Walworth		1					1
Waukesha: Mukernango			1				1
: Summit			1				1
Waupaca: Weyauwega				1			1

1 Blenheim
2 Esperance
3 Gilboa
4 Richmondville
5 Schoharie
6 Wright
T Total number of in-migrant families

the Town of Richmondville. The Village of Deposit (Town
of Stanford, Broome County) received three families from
Gilboa and three from Blenheim, a town contiguous to
Gilboa. All of the families that went to the City of
Albany settled in wards 9 or 10; fifteen of these eighteen
families had resided in the contiguous towns of Schoharie
(9), Esperance (3), and Wright (3). The seven families
that resided in 1860 at Lincoln, Illinois, the county seat
of Logan County, had been residents of the Town of Wright;
at least three of these families were related. The
majority of migrant families were, however, rather
dispersed, a suggestion that channelization was not a
significant factor in the pattern of total displacement
migration.

An alternative explanation is, however, more
likely. Channelization is both a temporal and a spatial
process (Roseman, 1971b). It is the result of decisions
to migrate from a given place to a specific destination
made over a long period of time. The cross-sectional
approach of this study is not likely to capture more than
one or two families who make up a small segment in any
given channel. A longitudinal approach is required to
test the channelization hypothesis.

The 1860 census manuscripts for the towns wherein
resided the seemingly isolated families do provide a
suggestion of the temporal dimension of this process.

Rarely was the recent migrant family from Schoharie County the only family with New York origins in the immediate vicinity. Two or three other families from the Empire State were always within a couple of manuscript census pages. Moreover, the surnames of some these families were common in Schoharie County. Those who migrated within New York State also were apparently not without friends or relatives at their new places of residence. The 1865 census manuscripts indicate that recent in-migrants were always within a few dwellings of earlier migrants born in Schoharie County.

Urbanward migration was a minor component in the pattern of total displacement migration. Only 24 families were found in the nearby cities of Albany and Schenectady and the urban town of Catskill. Among the families who migrated westward, only the seven who went to Lincoln, Illinois and the one who moved to suburban Chicago should be considered urbanward migrants. Four families went to Guilderland, a "suburban" town midway between Albany and Schenectady. One other went to suburban Philadelphia. If one considers the Town of Schoharie, with a village of 866 persons, an urbanward destination, the number of urbanward migrants increases considerably. Thirty-one families, nearly all from the contiguous Towns of Esperance and Wright, would be added to the list. The fact that most of the in-migrants to Albany and Schenectady were from the

Town of Schoharie suggests that urbanward migration within New York during the mid-1800s was stepwise.

Channelization was an important factor in urbanward migration. A gravity model for sixteen selected cities and urbanized towns of New York based upon migrant stock (the number of residents in 1855 born in Schoharie County) closely approximates the observed pattern of urbanward migration from 1855 to 1860 (Table 5.3). This model shows that the urban places that had demonstrated the greatest amount of interaction with Schoharie County by 1855 were those that received the greatest number of migrants from the study area in the period from 1855 to 1860. Earlier migrants from Schoharie County to all such places undoubtedly influenced the destination choices of those who later left Schoharie through regular contact with friends and relatives.

Few of the migrants found in the West went to urban places, but an unknown number of the 158 not traced may have done so. Cities were, according to Wade (1967:1), "the spearheads of the frontier." These nascent commercial and manufacturing centers commanded vast hinterlands in the rich mid-continent and it is reasonable to assume that these places would have attracted some of Schoharie's out-migrants. Rail and water carriers, the dominant modes of conveyance for migrants from New York during the 1850s, directed people into these burgeoning

TABLE 5.3

URBAN DESTINATIONS AND MIGRANT STOCK IN 1855

Place	Distance from Schoharie	Residents Born in Schoharie	Interaction Index(1)	In-migrant Families
Albany	35 m	362	.2955	18
Auburn*	112 m	25	.0020	0
Brooklyn*	136 m	52	.0028	0
Buffalo*	228 m	55	.0011	0
Catskill	40 m	88	.0550	2
Hudson	41 m	24	.0143	0
Kingston	52 m	30	.0111	0
New York City*	128 m	169	.0103	0
Oswego*	122 m	36	.0024	0
Poughkeepsie	70 m	12	.0024	0
Rochester*	169 m	67	.0023	0
Rome	70 m	64	.0131	0
Schenectady	30 m	42	.0467	4
Syracuse	94 m	78	.0088	0
Troy	42 m	47	.0266	0
Utica	55 m	95	.0314	0

* Nominal records of this place were not searched
1 Number of residents born in Schoharie (P) divided by the distance squared (D2) between the geographic centers of Schoharie County and each respective urban place.

mid-western cities. Many people may have seen the
opportunities for employment when they disembarked and
foregone the additional costs of venturing into the
"wilderness". Moreover, Schoharie's newspapers regularly
reprinted articles first published in the newspapers of
St. Louis, St. Paul, Chicago, Peoria, and Detroit, among
others. Perhaps the editors subscribed to mid-western
papers, but it also seems likely that former residents of
Schoharie sent copies of the local press back home. These
articles must have had some affect upon those who read
them.

The 158 families not found in either 1860 or 1865
may appear to be problematic but the census manuscripts of
every potential destination were not examined. Indices
for the 1860 census exist for only Wisconsin and
Minnesota. Other inter-state migrants were traced using
newspaper accounts as finding aids. Moreover, the records
for every conceiveable destination within New York State
were not examined. The 1865 census manuscripts, the key
finding aid for intra-state migrants, have been lost for
about forty percent of the state's populace. It is
possible therefore that channelized migration flows in
addition to those found did exist. The likely spatial
distribution of missing families in 1855 is suggestive of
this. Many such families appear to have been neighbors.
Groups of two or three missing families numbered

consecutively in the 1855 census manuscripts were not uncommon. The hypothesis of channelization should not be rejected without further study.

It is concluded that the observed pattern of out-migration from the six rural towns studied conforms to that expected. Families who made relatively short-distance moves were in the majority group. Return migration seems to have been a significant factor in this pattern. Longer distance migrants were in the minority. Most of these families left their rural homes in Schoharie County and settled in other rural places. Urbanward migrants were few in number, and most went to nearby cities that had in earlier years also been important destinations of out-migrants from Schoharie County. The sizeable number of total displacement migrants not traced suggests dispersed rather than channelized destinations, but longitudinal studies should be undertaken before this explanation of long-distance migration is challenged.

Moreover, given the representativeness of the sample population, it is clear that out-migrant families from rural areas of the northeastern United States did not abandon farms and shops for the factories and commerce of cities or the virgin soils of the distant frontier. Most out-migrant families who left any specific rural district moved only short-distances to other rural places. Families who went West or into cities were but a select

few of the out-migrants from rural places during the
mid-nineteenth century.

Differentials Among Out-Migrants

Differentials among out-migrants have yet to be
examined in studies of ninteenth century migration. Two
such analyses follow. The first explores the
socio-demographic and economic characteristics that
differentiate partial displacement migrants from total
displacement migrants. The 59 families who settled in the
zone of transition are excluded from this analysis. The
second analysis investigates differentials between
migrants to urban places and total displacement migrants
to rural places, It includes among the former the 31
partially displaced families who moved from contiguous
towns to the county seat town of Schoharie.

It is hypothesized that the socio-demographic and
economic characteristics that differentiated migrants from
non-migrants are also significant differentials among
out-migrants. Therefore, the variables tested in both
analyses are those elaborated in Chapter 4. Analysis is
undertaken using bivariate and multivariate techniques.
The former consists of Chi-square and student's t tests.
A significance level of .05 was adopted. Multivariate

analysis is accomplished with Multiple Classification
Analysis.

Partial and Total Displacement Differentials

Tilly and Brown (1967) suggest that several
different modes of social "auspices" govern migration.
Their study of contemporary urban in-migration found that
people of higher socio-economic status migrate under the
auspices of labor markets and formal networks, such as job
transfers. People of lesser socio-economic status usually
migrate under the auspices of kinship.

Although not explicitly spatial, the social
auspices model is suggestive of differentials between
partial and total displacement migrants. Since partial
displacement migrants are, by definition, families and
individuals who retain some elements of their former
activity spaces, they are expected to have stronger ties
with these former places of residence. Conversely, total
displacement migrants should have weaker ties. Among
these ties are prior migration experience, duration of
residence, number of kinfolk, and ownership of real
property.

Economic differentials between partial and total
displacement migrants should also be evident. Since

higher status jobs are fewer in number and distributed less ubiquitously, people engaged in higher status jobs are more likely to be total displacement migrants.

Bivariate Analyses

Statistical analysis indicates that only five socio-demographic and economic characteristics differed between the 206 partial displacement migrants and 257 total displacement migrants (Table 5.4).(2) These five were the number of children in families headed by males aged 30-34 and 35-39, landownership, occupation, socio-economic rank, and national origin.

In terms of their life-cycle characteristics, partial displacement migrants were very much like total displacement migrants. They were only one year older, heads of almost identically sized families, and had the same number of children. The latter was true in most instances regardless of the age of the family head. However, total displacement migrants between the ages of 30 and 34 did have significantly fewer children under ten years of age than partial displacement migrants. Total displacement migrants aged 35-39 also had significantly fewer children aged 5-9 years than partial displacement migrants. This suggests that individuals aged 30-39 with large families may have moved to satisfy housing needs and

TABLE 5.4

BIVARIATE ANALYSES OF PARTIAL AND TOTAL DISPLACEMENT MIGRATION DIFFERENTIALS

CHARACTERISTIC	N	test	X2	MEANS		Sig Level
				PDM	TDM	
Life-cycle characteristics						
Age	465	t	-	37.69	36.72	.340
Family Size	465	t	-	5.07	5.09	.949
Children 0-4 years of age	465	t	-	.93	.86	.467
Head age 30-34	465	t	-	1.43	1.04	.028*
Children 5-9 years of age	465	t	-	.74	.60	.087
Head aged 30-34	465	t	-	1.00	.63	.034*
Head aged 34-39	465	t	-	1.12	.67	.024*
Place ties						
Previous Migration Experience	465	X2	3.27	-	-	.071
Duration of Residence (1)	370	t	-	8.63	8.03	.625
Kinship - number of						
same-surnamed persons	465	t	-	13.30	11.15	.074
same-surnamed heads	465	t	-	2.59	2.21	.075
Landownership	465	X2	7.75	-	-	.005*
Economic condition						
Occupation	465	X2	49.41	-	-	.000*
Economic Rank	456	t	-	$245.16	$336.34	.003*
Other socio-demographics						
Race	465	X2	insufficient cell size			
National Origin						
USA (1) / Foreign	372	X2	22.06	-	-	.000*
German/Irish/British (2)/Other	73	X2	insufficient cell size			

* Significant at the .05 level.
1. Does not include natives of the town of enumeration in 1855.
2. English, Welsh, and Scottish.

that same-aged individuals with small families may have migrated in response to perceived distant opportunities.

Three measures of place ties, previous migration experience, duration of residence among non-natives, and kinship, were not significant differentials, but landownership was. People without land were one and one-half times more likely to be total displacement migrants than partial displacement migrants. Landowners were equally represented in both groups.

Both measures of economic condition, occupation and economic rank, were important differentials. Individuals employed in the professions or engaged as proprietors, clerks, or civil servants were significantly more likely to be total displacement migrants than partial displacement migrants (Table 5.5). Most likely to remain in close proximity to their previous homes were farmers. The economic rank of total displacement migrants was also significantly above that of partial displacement migrants. The per family dwelling value of the former was $336.34. That of the latter was $245.16. This suggests that total displacement migrants had greater financial resources at their disposal than did partial displacement migrants and that the former could afford the greater cost of a long-distance relocation.

Nativity was also an important differential. Individuals born outside the United States were

TABLE 5.5

OCCUPATION AS A DIFFERENTIAL
BETWEEN PARTIAL AND TOTAL DISPLACEMENT MIGRANTS (1)
in percentages

Occupation	N	PDMs	TDMs
Learned Professions	18	5.6	94.4
Businessmen, Clerks, and Civil Servants	33	15.2	84.8
Craftsmen	108	35.2	64.8
Farmers	206	59.2	40.8
Semi-skilled Workers, and Laborers	57	42.1	57.9
No occupation reported	43	27.9	72.1

1. Occupational categories are found in Appendix F.

considerably more likely to be total displacement migrants than partial displacement migrants. Among the foreign-born those born in Germany or Ireland were more likely to be total displacement migrants.

Farmers

The variables concerning farm size and value were examined for those who called themselves farmers (Table 5.6). Only one differential, value per acre, was significant. Partial displacement migrants had farmed property valued at $24.25 per acre, slightly less than twice the value of that farmed by total displacement migrants. The latter appear to have cultivated poorer soils and probably had greater difficulty in sustaining themselves. Perhaps their out-migration was a response to the "push" of this relatively "hostile" environment and the "pull" of perceived fertility of soils elsewhere.

Summary

Bivariate analyses have shown that partial displacement migrants and total displacement migrants differed in some of their socio-demographic and economic characteristics. In general, the latter were associated with fewer children under ten years of age, landlessness,

TABLE 5.6

DIFFERENTIALS BETWEEN PARTIAL AND TOTAL DISPLACEMENT OUT-MIGRANT FARMERS

CHARACTERISTIC	N	TEST	X2	MEANS		SIG LEVEL
				PDMS.	TDMS.	
Life-cycle characteristics						
Age	203	t	—	37.47	38.26	.633
Family Size	203	t	—	5.05	5.33	.360
Children 0-4 years of age	203	t	—	.87	.88	.958
Place ties						
Previous Migration Experience	201	X2	.06	—	—	.807
Duration of Residence (1)	152	t	—	9.84	10.17	.890
Kinship – same-surnamed persons	203	t	—	13.87	14.57	.731
– same-surnamed heads	203	t	—	2.76	2.90	.702
Landownership	203	X2	.04	—	—	.830
Economic condition						
Economic Rank	203	t	—	$220.39	$289.07	.105
Other socio-demographics						
Nativity: USA (1) / Foreign	152	X2	10.05	—	—	.002*
Agricultural characteristics						
Improved acreage	203	t	—	39.32	45.42	.380
Unimproved acreage	203	t	—	16.60	23.44	.144
Total acreage	203	t	—	55.92	68.86	.189
Percentage improved acreage	203	t	—	46.42	41.70	.385
Value of farmland	203	t	—	$1317.87	$1434.18	.617
Value of livestock	203	t	—	$ 254.44	$ 267.67	.753
Value of agricultural implements	203	t	—	$ 63.69	$ 70.56	.548
Total value	203	t	—	$1636.00	$1772.41	.623
Value per acre of farmland	203	t	—	$ 24.25	$ 13.85	.028*

* Significant at the .05 level.
1. Does not include natives of the town of enumeration in 1855.

higher skilled occupations, greater economic rank, and foreign places of birth. All other characteristics analyzed were not significant differentials.

Multivariate Analysis

Four differentials found to be significant among all out-migrants were evaluated using Multiple Classification Analysis (Table 5.7). These were 1) whether or not the head was a landowner, 2) his occupation, 3) the family's economic rank, and 4) nativity of the family head. These four factors explained 20 of the variation in migration behavior of the sample population.

Results of this MCA are both informative and, in one respect surprising. Higher skilled individuals were, as expected, more likely to be total displacement migrants than partial displacement migrants. Farmers were least likely to migrate. Nativity was a significant differential. German and Irish born residents were less likely to remain in close proximity to their towns of residence in 1855 than other foreign born residents and those born in the United States. People residing in the poorest and in the highest valued homes were more likely to be total displacement migrants than partial displacement migrants. These three variables were

TABLE 5.7

MCA OF DIFFERENTIALS BETWEEN
PARTIAL AND TOTAL DISPLACEMENT MIGRANTS

Variable + Category	N	Unadjusted DEV"N	ETA	Adjusted for Independents DEV"N	BETA
Landownership					
0 Does not own land	281	.06		-.00	
1 Owns land	209	-.08		.01	
			.14		.01
Occupational Category					
1 Learned Professions	14	.33		.33	
2 Business, Civil Serv	34	.26		.30	
3 Craftsmen	111	.06		.07	
4 Farmers	203	-.18		-.16	
5 Semi-skilled, Labor	56	-.01		-.09	
6 No occupation report	72	.24		.20	
			.36		.34
Economic Rank					
1 Lowest Quintile	134	.01		.01	
2 Second Quintile	124	.03		.02	
3 Middle Quintile	96	-.12		-.09	
4 Fourth Quintile	56	-.08		-.05	
5 Highest Quintile	80	.14		.11	
			.17		.13
Nativity					
1 Census Town Native	100	-.07		-.06	
2 Other USA	313	-.04		-.04	
3 German	23	.32		.35	
4 Irish	42	.31		.29	
5 Other Foreign	12	-.10		-.06	
			.25		.25

Multiple R Squared   .200
Multiple R   .448
Grand Mean =   1.60

reasonably independent of each other. Their Eta and Beta values were virtually unchanged when testing for intercorrelations. Landownership was, on the other hand, highly correlated with the other three factors. Its explanatory power was virtually erased when the other three factors were entered into the model simultaneously. Landownership, probably the most powerful differential between non-migrants and migrants and between persisters and non-persisters in other studies of migration during the 1800s, appears to have been a relatively unimportant differential among out-migrants. It appears that the distance migrated by those who left the study area can be explained almost entirely by occupation, economic rank, and national origin.

Farmers

A somewhat different view of migration behavior is presented by the Multiple Classification Analysis of differentials among out-migrant farmers (Table 5.8). Nearly 17 percent of the variation in behavior is explained in a model that incorporated landownership, economic rank, farm value per acre, and nativity. Nativity exhibited virtually the same effect as before, but the number of foreign born individuals is quite small. The explanatory power of economic rank was nearly twice

TABLE 5.8

MCA OF DIFFERENTIALS BETWEEN
PARTIAL AND TOTAL DISPLACEMENT OUT-MIGRANT FARMERS

Variable + Category	N	Unadjusted DEV"N	ETA	Adjusted for Independents DEV"N	BETA
Landownership					
0 Does not own land	73	-.02		-.06	
1 Owns land	130	.01		.04	
			.03		.10
Economic Rank					
1 Lowest Quintile	60	.04		.01	
2 Second Quintile	47	.03		.05	
3 Middle Quintile	48	-.16		-.17	
4 Fourth Quintile	25	-.01		-.02	
5 Highest Quintile	23	.19		.24	
			.22		.24
Farm Value Per Aacre					
1 No value given	76	.01		-.00	
2 .25 to 15.99	36	.09		.11	
3 $16 to 25.00	38	.11		.13	
4 25.01 to 37.40	25	-.21		-.18	
5 37.41 to highest	28	-.09		-.15	
			.21		.23
Nativity					
1 Census Town Native	50	-.01		-.04	
2 Other USA	132	-.05		-.05	
3 German	6	.42		.46	
4 Irish	11	.40		.41	
5 Other Foreign	4	.09		.18	
			.26		.27

Multiple R Squared   .167
Multiple R   .409
Grand Mean = 1.41

that found in the model for all migrants. The greater likelihood of middle quintile individuals moving and highest quintile individuals migrating was the reason for this. Farm value per acre was nearly as important as economic rank and national origin. Individuals for whom data were not available because they were not enumerated in the agricultural schedule were almost equally divided between partial displacement migrants and total displacement migrants. Those with property valued at less than $25 were more likely to be total displacement migrants. Those with property valued above $25 were more likely to be partial displacement migrants. Moreover, in contrast to the MCA of all occupational groups, landownership was an important differential. Its explanatory power was, in fact, trebled, not diminished, when intercorrelation with the three independent variables was controlled. It appears that landownership was an important differential only among farmers, the group most directly dependent upon the soil for their livelihood.

Urban and Rural Differentials

Although there have been no studies of whether the socio-demographic and economic characteristics of urbanward migrants differed from those of migrants to rural areas during the nineteenth century, one may intuitively suspect that, at least with respect to occupation, these two groups of migrants differed significantly. Those engaged in the learned professions, business, civil service, and crafts were probably more likely to settle in cities where their skills were presumably in greater demand. So, too, were semi-skilled and unskilled laborers. Mechanization of agriculture undoubtedly affected the demand for their casual services, and cities offered a better prospect for regular, non-seasonal work than did the countryside. Farmers, especially those who were relatively prosperous, were probably among those least likely to settle in cities. They probably considered themselves to be competent farmers, and may have felt that migration into cities was an admission of failure. Hard times might have been blamed on soil quality or drouth, or other vagaries of weather, and not on their skill as cultivators. Farmers were, then, likely to migrate to other rural places where agricultural prospects were perceived to be better. The life-cycle charactertics, place ties, economic conditions other than occupation, and other socio-demographics including race and national origin are not expected to differ between migrants to urban and to rural destinations.

Statistical analyses indicate that the characteristics of 67 urbanward migrants differed from those of 69 migrants with rural destinations in only two rspects: occupation and the number of children less than five years of age (Table 5.9). Upperclass/higher skilled individuals were, as hypothesized, more likely to migrate to cities (Table 5.10). So, too, were semi-skilled and unskilled laborers. Among those for whom an occupation was reported, farmers were the least represented among urbanward migrants.

Migrants to urban places were also likely to have fewer children less than five years of age. This may be related to the occupational distribution of urbanward migrants (see Chapter 2 discussion of urbanization and fertility). Farmers were likely to have more children as a means of acquiring unpaid labor. The fact that family size was also not significant is explained by the greater probability of augmentation and extension of the nuclear family among upper income and lesser income families, respectively.

Totally Displaced Urban and Rural Migrants

Two additional characteristics, previous migration experience and kinship, are also significant if the 31 families who moved from the Towns of Esperance and Wright to the contiguous Town of Schoharie are excluded from the analyses (Table 5.11). Individuals without previous

TABLE 5.9

BIVARIATE ANALYSES OF DIFFERENTIALS BETWEEN URBAN AND RURAL MIGRANTS

CHARACTERISTIC	N	TEST	X2	MEANS URBAN	MEANS RURAL	SIG LEVEL
Life-cycle characteristics						
Age	136	t	–	37.22	35.39	.273
Family Size	136	t	–	5.19	5.62	.346
Children 0-4 years of age	136	t	–	.64	1.07	.004*
Children 5-9 years of age	136	t	–	.54	.80	.078
Place ties						
Previous Migration Experience	95	X2	3.08	–	–	.079
Duration of Residence (1)	95	t	–	7.90	8.02	.958
Kinship – number of						
same-surnamed persons	136	t	–	12.03	14.65	.233
same-surnamed heads	136	t	–	2.43	2.71	.502
Landownership	136	X2	0.00	–	–	.000*
Economic condition						
Occupation	136	X2	15.63	–	–	.008*
Economic Rank	133	t	–	$374.44	$365.73	.887
Other socio-demographics						
Race	136	X2	insufficient cell size			
Nativity						
USA (1) / Foreign	95	X2	.939	–	–	.333
German/Irish/British (2)/Other	43	X2	insufficient cell size			

* Significant at the .05 level.
1. Does not include natives of the town of enumeration in 1855.
2. English, Welsh, and Scottish.

TABLE 5.10

OCCUPATION AS A DIFFERENTIAL
BETWEEN MIGRANTS TO URBAN AND RURAL PLACES (1)
in percentages

Occupation	N	Urban	Rural
Learned Professions	5	60.0	40.0
Businessmen, Clerks, and Civil Servants	16	68.8	31.3
Craftsmen	47	55.3	44.7
Farmers	44	34.1	65.9
Laborers and Semi-skilled workers	13	76.9	23.1
No occupation reported	11	18.2	81.8

1 Occupational categories are found in Appendix F.

TABLE 5.11

DIFFERENTIALS BETWEEN 36 URBAN AND 69 RURAL TOTAL DISPLACEMENT MIGRANTS

CHARACTERISTIC	N	TEST	X2	MEANS		SIG LEVEL
				URBAN	RURAL	
Life-cycle characteristics						
Age	107	t	–	37.36	35.39	.332
Family Size	107	t	–	5.67	5.62	.949
Children 0-4 years of age	107	t	–	.64	1.07	.015*
Children 5-9 years of age	107	t	–	.47	.80	.066
Place ties						
Previous Migration Experience	43	X2	3.99	–	–	.046*
Duration of Residence (1)	41	t	–	9.90	8.02	.502
Kinship – number of						
same-surnamed persons	107	t	–	9.94	14.65	.039*
same-surnamed heads	107	t	–	2.06	2.71	.137
Landownership	107	X2	0.00	–	–	1.000
Economic condition						
Occupation	105	X2	23.71	–	–	.000*
Economic Rank	102	t	–	$492.00	$365.73	.129
Other socio-demographics						
Race	107	X2	insufficient cell size			
Nativity						
USA (1) / Foreign	43	X2	.08	–	–	.782
German/Irish/British (2)/Other	12	X2	insufficient cell size			

* Significant at the .05 level.
1. Does not include natives of the town of enumeration in 1855.
2. English, Welsh, and Scottish.

migration experience were more than four times more likely to migrate to rural places than urban places (81.3 percent vs. 18.8 percent). Those with previous migration experience were less than one and one-half times more likely to behave similarly (58.9 percent vs. 41.1 percent). Given the transportation system it seems possible that many of the in-migrants to Schoharie County went through one or more urban places before settling in the county. Perhaps they acquired favorable images of cities in general that help explain their significant tendency to chose urban rather than rural destinations. The significance of kinship, as measured by the number of same surnamed persons residing in the towns of enumeration, is probably related to the fertility differentials noted above and not an independent effect on migration behavior.

Farmers

The characteristics of the 15 farmers who migrated to non-contiguous urban places were, in most respects, not significantly different from those of the 29 farmers who went to rural places (Table 5.12). Urbanward migrant farmers had smaller farms and less unimproved acreage.

TABLE 5.12
DIFFERENTIALS BETWEEN 15 URBAN AND 29 RURAL OUT-MIGRANT FARMERS

CHARACTERISTIC	N	TEST	X2	MEANS URBAN	MEANS RURAL	SIG LEVEL
Life-cycle characteristics						
Age	44	t	–	40.87	34.93	.207
Family Size	44	t	–	4.67	5.48	.184
Children 0-4 years of age	44	t	–	.47	1.03	.030*
Children 5-9 years of age	44	t	–	.53	.72	.428
Place ties						
Previous Migration Experience	24	X2	1.45	–	–	.228
Duration of Residence (1)	24	t	–	4.00	11.78	.108
Kinship – same-surnamed persons	44	t	–	17.40	16.90	.931
– same-surnamedheads	44	t	–	3.53	3.21	.765
Landownership	44	X2	0.00	–	–	1.000
Economic condition						
Economic Rank	44	t	–	$348.30	$321.61	.779
Other socio-demographics						
Nativity: USA (1) / Foreign	24	X2		insufficient cell size		
German/Irish/British (2)/Other	2	X2		insufficient cell size		
Agricultural characteristics						
Improved acreage	44	t	–	36.58	53.96	.234
Unimproved acreage	44	t	–	10.67	34.71	.023*
Total acreage	44	t	–	47.25	88.67	.036*
Percentage improved acreage	44	t	–	51.95	46.44	.664
Value of farmland	44	t	–	$1763.67	$1581.90	.744
Value of livestock	44	t	–	$ 228.73	$ 308.79	.339
Value of agricultural implements	44	t	–	$ 51.67	$ 89.76	.096
Total value	44	t	–	$2044.07	$1980.45	.922
Value per acre of farmland	44	t	–	$ 29.26	$ 15.35	.165

* Significant at the .05 level.
1. Does not include natives of the town of enumeration in 1855.
2. English, Welsh, and Scottish.

This suggests that urbanward farmers were dissatisfied with the income earned in agriculture.

Summary

It is clear that the behavior of rural out-migrants during the mid-1800s is remarkably similar to that expected given existing migration theory and recent empirical studies. The out-migration field was dominated by short-distance migrants the majority of whom were partial displacement migrants. Channelization is evident in the behavior of total displacement migrants, especially those to urban places. The differentials among out-migrants were also those expected. Among the more important differentials between partial displacement migrants and total displacement migrants were occupation, economic rank, and national origin. Occupation was the most important differential between rural and urbanward migrants.

Notes

1. I did not seek those I believed to be recently formed families (a wife who would have been less than 27 years of age in 1850 and either no children or children less than 3 years of age in 1855). Moreover, I did not seek those whose place of residence in 1850 as indicated by their birthplaces and those of their children was likely to have been outside New York and the New England States or those with common names --- listings of more than 20 in any given index.

2. Two partial displacement migrants and six total
displacement migrants who resided in institutional
dwellings (hotels, boarding houses, dormitories, school
residence halls, etc.) were excluded from the analyses of
partial displacement migrants and total displacement
migrants for two reasons. First, the dwelling value
reported was often in the thousands of dollars and the
variable "economic rank" would be skewed accordingly.
Second, their unusual living arrangements made them
atypical residents.

CHAPTER 6

CONCLUSION

This study has investigated the migration behavior
of approximately 2,000 family groups who were resident in
rural areas of New York in 1855. It had three substantive
objectives. First, the process of migration selectivity
was investigated by examining differentials between
non-migrants and migrants with common origins. Second,
the out-migration field was examined and the destinations
of rural out-migrants were documented. Third,
differentials among out-migrants categorized by distance
migrated and by type of destination was analyzed.

These issues have not been addressed previously.
Nominal data sources commonly utilized in studies of
population persistence and migration do not lend
themselves readily to the study of out-migration because
destinations are not reported. Linking these data sources
required development of an exhaustive, replicable
methodology that permitted fuller decomposition of the
sample population than that attempted by other scholars.
Less than eight percent of the male heads of families
determined to be survivors from 1855 to 1860 were not
positively located in situ or in their new places of
residence.

The remarkably high recovery rate associated with this methodology is encouraging. Other researchers will be able to apply these procedures and determine the whereabouts of their sample populations. No longer should social historians be satisfied with comparisons of persisters and and non-persisters. Fuller decomposition of the latter will result in more studies of non-migrants and out-migrants, of short-distance migrants and longer-distance migrants, and of urbanward migrants and migrants to rural locales. Research that explores these differentials will contribute significantly to knowledge of migration processes and result in heightened understanding of the impact of migration on population change.

Previous studies of population persistence in the United States during the nineteenth century are lacking in two respects. First, they have not distiguished migrants from other non-persisters has rendered conclusions about differentials between non-migrants and migrants tentative. Moreover, most of these works have not sought to build upon the existing body of theoretical and empirical migration literature. To some extent this may be related to the populations sampled. The emphasis of social historians, in particular, has been place, not process. The communities studied and the residents sampled have not been selected because they were representative of the national, regional, or state population. Thus, generalizations about the migration behavior of North Americans during the nineteenth century, and the applicability of general migration theory to that behavior, have not been offered.

This research specifically addressed these concerns. The study area was selected because it was typical of rural New York in 1855. The sample population was almost fully decomposed using techniques detailed in Chapter 3. The migration behavior expected was based upon the existing theoretical literature and empirical studies.

This study found that most of the hypothesized differentials between non-migrant and out-migrants heads of families were significant. Although life-cycle characteristics (age, family size, and the number of children aged 0-4 years) and other socio-demographic factors (nativity, in particular) were important differentials (see Table 4.1) the typical out-migrant family was most readily distinguished from the typical non-migrant family by place ties and economic condition. The head of an out-migrant family usually owned no land, was related to only one or two other heads of families resident in the study area, and was probably a European immigrant who had in-migrated within the past five years or so. He was most likely engaged in an occupation other than farming and he and his family resided in a dwelling valued at about \$325. Conversely, the head of a typical non-migrant family was a native of the town of enumeration in 1855 or a long-time resident (15-25 years), American-born, a member of a large kinship network, and a landowner. He was probably engaged in farming and he and his family resided in a house valued at about \$425.

These same differentials were significant among farmers, the largest occupational group. Additionally, the typical non-migrant farmer operated a farm that was roughly one and one-half times the size and value of that operated by the typical out-migrant farmer. These findings support the general hypotheses that associate migration behavior with life-cycle characteristics, place ties, and economic condition.

The observed out-migration field was dominated by short distance or partial displacement migration. Most people did not abandon their homes in the rural Northeast and migrate to cities or the frontier. The majority moved short distances to nearby rural places. This finding challenges the traditional interpretation of a close association between rural emigration and depopulation and migration to cities and the western frontier.

Whereas the spatial pattern of the out-migration field conformed to the expected pattern, the differentials associated with distance migrated and the destination type varied in some respects from those hypothesized.

Life-cycle characteristics and place ties generally were not significant differentials (see Table 5.4). Only among heads of families aged 30-39 was the number of children less than ten years of age an important differential. Large families were more likely to migrate short-distance than longer-distances. Economic condition, as measured by occupation and economic rank, and other socio-demographics, specifically national origin, were the most important distance differentials. Those who had farmed in 1855 were more more likely to out-migrate short-distances from their towns of residence in 1855. Longer-distance migration was associated with those in higher-status occupations and those who lived in higher valued homes. Most of these longer-distance migrant families were also headed by foreign-born males.

Occupation was the most important differential between urbanward migrants and those who went to rural places (see Tables 5.9, 5.10, and 5.11). Farmers and those who reported no occupation went to rural places; those in the learned professions or business and those who were unskilled laborers went to urban areas. Moreover, urbanward migrants tended to be slightly older and to have fewer children than did those who went to rural places. They were also more likely to have migrated previously.

These findings suggest that perceptions of economic and social opportunity were the most important forces at work in the decision where to migrate. Once the decision to migrate had been made, the influence of ties to the place of residence in 1855 appears to have been unimportant. The possible places of employment for those engaged in higher status and skilled occupations were fewer and farther apart than for other occupational groups. The foreign-born, having unsuccessfully attempted to form bonds within their respective towns of residence, may have considered other nearby rural places to be similarly "closed" to outsiders. The differentials between partial displacement migrants and total displacement migrants are a reflection, then, of the limited opportunities for both social and economic advancement in rural areas. People who sought advancement probably recognized that they could not do so by remaining close to their places of residence in 1855 because these places were likely to be too similar in their economic and social structures. Peopling the cities and the frontier was left, perhaps, to families headed by more ambitious individuals. Those who were left behind, be they non-migrants or partial displacement migrants, were, therefore, those who had become part of the community and were economically and socially content and those who lacked the financial resources and self-confidence to seek opportunities in unfamiliar areas.

APPENDIX A

OCCUPATIONS OF SCHOHARIE COUNTY RESIDENTS IN 1855

TYPE, Activity	NUMBER
LEARNED PROFESSIONS	
Civil engineer	2
Clergyman	42
Dentist	4
Engineer	1
Lawyer	39
Nurse	1
Physician	68
Surveyor	1
BUSINESSMEN, CLERKS	
Agents	3
Baker	2
Boarding House keeper	4
Brewer, distiller	2
Cattle dealer	1
Clerks, copyists	60
Clothiers	15
Cotton manufacturer	1
Dealers	4
Gardners, florists	1
Grocers	8
Hotel, innkeeper	42
Manufacturer	2
Marble dealer	1
Merchants	138
Millers	61
Pedlers	22
Photographer	3
Portrait painter	2
Speculator	1
Stage proprietor	1
Tobacconist	1
CIVIL SERVANTS	
Civil officers	7
Inspector	1
Keeper, warden	1
Mail agent	1
Post master	1
Teacher	160

CRAFTSMEN
Agricultural implement makers	11
Barbers	2
Basketbakers	9
Blacksmith	160
Blockmakers	19
Brickmakers	2
Broommakers	2
Butchers	10
Cabinetmakers	39
Carpenters	379
Clockmakers	1
Coach, wagonmakers	78
Combmakers	1
Coopers	81
Dressmakers	41
Engravers	1
Gold, silversmiths	2
Gunsmith	1
Hat, cap makers	12
Jewellers	4
Machinists	13
Mason	81
Mechanics	21
Milliners	53
Millwrights	10
Moulders	1
Painters, graziers	33
Papermakers	7
Piano maker	1
Printers	10
Saddle, harnessmakers	32
Sash and blind maker	1
Sawyers	3
Shoemakers	161
Shinglemakers	4
Stone, marble cutters	2
Tailors	147
Tanners	28
Tinsmiths	18
Trimmers	4
Toy and fancy maker	1
Turners	1
Umbrella maker	3
Watchmakers	3
Weaver	12
Wheelwrights	1

FARMERS	5372
LABORERS	1613

SERVICE WORKERS
    Bar keepers   3
    Drivers, coachmen   9
    Drovers   1
    Furnacemen   11
    Gate keepers   5
    Hunters   1
    Laundress   3
    Lime burners   1
    Railroad employees   2
    Sailors, boatmen   4
    Servants   74
    Teamsters, carters, draymen   10
    Watchmen   1

MISCELLANEOUS
    Apprentices   3
    Students   43

Source: Hough, 1857:178-195.

APPENDIX B

COMPARATIVE MORTALITY ESTIMATES BY COHORT AND GENDER,
IN NEW YORK STATE AND SCHOHARIE COUNTY,
1855-1860 (1)

NEW YORK STATE MALES

Age	L(x)	5Q(x)	Est. Deaths
0-1	51,440	139.42	7,171.76
1-4	186,368	70.84	13,202.31
5-9	198,742	20.59	4,092.10
10-14	189,298	14.91	2,822.43
15-19	170,015	21.92	3,726.73
20-24	168,114	31.13	5,233.39
25-29	158,547	34.12	5,409.62
30-34	140,355	39.10	5,487.88
35-39	111,489	46.44	5,177.55
40-44	93,297	57.52	5,366.44
45-49	72,949	71.21	5,194.70
50-59	100,985	109.56	11,063.92
60-69	53,825	207.76	11,182.68
70-79	22,462	400.08	8,986.60
80+	6,661	1000.00	6,661.00
	1,724,547		100,779.00

Death Rate = 58.44

1 Estimated from Coale and Demeny (1960),
Level 13, West.

NEW YORK STATE FEMALES

Age	L(x)	5Q(x)	Est. Deaths
0-1	51,082	118.31	6,043.51
1-4	182,729	71.69	13,099.84
5-9	195,639	21.36	4,178.85
10-14	185,252	16.59	3,073.33
15-19	188,927	22.61	4,271.64
20-24	195,100	28.86	5,630.59
25-29	166,530	32.66	5,438.87
30-34	134,234	37.04	4,972.03
35-39	103,409	41.51	4,292.51
40-44	86,960	46.44	4,038.42
45-49	65,453	53.76	3,518.76
50-59	95,817	83.49	7,999.76
60-69	54,215	169.01	9,162.88
70-79	22,555	354.03	7,985.15
80+	7,236	1000.00	7,236.00
	1,735,138		90,942.00

Death Rate = 52.41

1 Estimated from Coale and Demeny (1960),
Level 13, West.

SCHOHARIE COUNTY MALES

Age	L(x)	5Q(x)	Est. Deaths
0-1	470	139.42	65.5
1-4	1,897	70.84	134.4
5-9	2,195	20.59	45.2
10-14	2,072	14.91	30.9
15-19	1,772	21.92	38.8
20-24	1,428	31.13	44.5
25-29	1,232	34.12	42.0
30-34	1,138	39.10	44.5
35-39	964	46.44	44.8
40-44	860	57.52	49.5
45-49	687	71.21	48.9
50-59	1,040	109.56	113.9
60-69	663	207.76	137.7
70-79	318	400.08	127.2
80+	85	1000.00	85.0
	16,821		1052.8

Death Rate = 62.59

1 Estimated from Coale and Demeny (1960),
Level 13, West.

SCHOHARIE COUNTY FEMALES

Age	L(x)	5Q(x)	Est. Deaths
0-1	447	118.31	52.9
1-4	1,810	71.69	129.8
5-9	2,133	21.36	45.6
10-14	2,057	16.59	34.1
15-19	1,787	22.61	40.4
20-24	1,526	28.86	44.0
25-29	1,305	32.66	42.6
30-34	1,124	37.04	41.6
35-39	943	41.51	39.1
40-44	804	46.44	37.3
45-49	693	53.76	37.3
50-59	1,006	83.49	84.0
60-69	658	169.01	111.2
70-79	286	354.03	101.3
80+	103	1000.00	103.0
	16,682		944.2

Death Rate = 56.60

1 Estimated from Coale and Demeny (1960), Level 13, West.

APPENDIX C

PART 1: DATA FORMAT AND CODES

CARD NO.	COLUMN NO.	VARIABLE NAME
1	1	CNUM1,
		Card 1 of 5
1	3-8	CASEID1,
		Six digit number unique to this case
1	10-13	SURNAM1,
		First four letters of surname
1	14-17	SURNAM2,
		Second four letters of surname
1	18-21	FORNAM,
		First four letters of forename
1	23-24	AGE55,
		Age in 1855 in whole years
		(00) infant less than one year old
		(-9) missing data
1	25	GENDER,
		Gender
		(1) male
		(2) female
1	26	RACE,
		Racial group
		(1) white
		(2) black
		(3) mulatto
1	27-28	REL55,
		Relationship to head of family group
		(00) unspecified
		(10) head
		(21) husband
		(22) wife
		(31) son
		(32) daughter
		(33) brother
		(34) sister
		(35) father
		(36) mother
		(37) step-son
		(38) step-daughter
		(41) grandson
		(42) granddaughter
		(43) grandson-in-law
		(44) granddaughter-in-law
		(45) grandfather
		(46) grandmother

```
                    (51)  nephew
                    (52)  neice
                    (53)  male cousin
                    (54)  female cousin
                    (55)  uncle
                    (56)  aunt
                    (61)  great-nephew
                    (62)  great-neice
                    (63)  great-uncle
                    (64)  great-aunt
                    (71)  great-grandson
                    (72)  great-granddaughter
                    (73)  adopted son
                    (74)  adopted daughter
                    (75)  half brother
                    (76)  half sister
                    (77)  step-father
                    (78)  step-mother
                    (81)  son-in-law
                    (82)  daughter-in-law
                    (83)  brother-in-law
                    (84)  sister-in-law
                    (85)  father-in-law
                    (86)  mother-in-law
                    (87)  grandmother-in-law
                    (88)  sister-in-law's child
                    (91)  employee, servant, domestic
                    (92)  lodger, boarder
                    (93)  unspecified
                    (94)  apprentice
                    (95)  laborer, farm or otherwise
                    (96)  child of employee or laborer
                    (97)  child of lodger
                    (98)  inmate, prisoner
                    (99)  tenant
1      29    MRSTT55,
                    Marital Status in 1855
                    (2)  currently married
                    (3)  widowed
                    (4)  divorced
1      30-31 DRRZ,
                    Consecutive years residence in this town
                    (98)  incorrectly reported
                    (99)  unknown, missing data
```

```
CARD   COLUMN   VARIABLE
NO.    NO.      NAME

 1     32       OCAT5,
                Occupational category
                (0) no occupation reported
                (1) learned professions
                (2) business, civil service
                (3) craftsmen
                (4) farmers
                (5) semi-skilled workers,
                    laborers, and service workers
 1     33-35    OCC55,
                Occupation in 1855
                (111) Lawyer
                (121) Physician
                (122) Dentist
                (123) Doctor
                (124) Physician & surgeon
                (125) Homeopathic physician
                (126) Nurse
                (131) Civil engineer
                (132) Geologist
                (133) Surveyor
                (134) Railroad contractor
                (151) Clergy
                (152) Minister
                (153) Reverend doctor
                (161) Banker
                (211) General merchandise
                (213) Clothier
                (214) Hardware
                (215) Druggist
                (216) Grocer
                (219) Grain merchant
                (221) Agricultural implement manufacturer
                (222) Leather goods manufacturer
                (223) Clothing manufacturer
                (225) Wagon manufacturer
                (227) Carriage manufacturer
                (228) Sash & blind manufacturer
                (230) Real estate and insurance
                (231) Dealer in patent wright
                (232) Speculator
                (233) Dealer
```

```
(241) Judge, Justice of the peace
(242) Mail contractor
(243) Sheriff
(244) School teacher
(246) Constables
(247) Fireman
(248) Poorhouse keeper
(249) Inspector of public works
(251) Barber
(252) Nurseryman
(253) Miller
(255) Marble dealer
(256) Stage proprietor
(261) Restauranter
(262) Rooming house
(263) Hotel operator
(264) Innkeeper
(266) Beer peddlar
(267) Segar -cigar- maker
(271) Principal of private academy
(272) Steward of private academy
(273) Teacher in private academy
(274) College teacher
(275) School teacher
(276) Music teacher
(277) Writing teacher
(278) Ornamental teacher
(279) School administrator
(299) Fanning mill maker
(310) Farmer who owns land
(320) Farmer without land
(330) Bee keeper
(351) Sawyer
(352) Lumberman
(353) Lumbering
(360) AgricultureLl-sIil-tEeraturst
(411) Traveling salesman
(412) Traveling merchant
(413) Peddlar
(414) Tin peddlar
(420) Bookkeeper, accountant
(431)_ Bank clerk
(432) Merchant´s clerk
(441) Cotton mill agent
(471) Expressman
(472) Mail carrier
```

```
(511)  Jeweler
(512)  Watchmaker
(513)  Printer
(514)  Clockmaker
(515)  Gunsmith
(516)  Paper making
(517)  Silversmith
(518)  Engraver
(519)  Degar artist -Deugarotypes-
(521)  Shoemaking
(522)  Tannery foreman
(524)  Cordwain
(527)  Harness maker
(531)  Tailor
(532)  Dressmaker
(533)  Seamstress
(534)  Hatter
(535)  Milliner -lady's hats-
(536)  Weaver
(537)  Milliner & dressmaker
(541)  Tinsmith
(542)  Blacksmith
(543)  Silverplater
(544)  Silver burnisher
(545)  Tinner
(546)  Silversmith
(547)  Tinman
(548)  Pill box maker
(551)  Cooper
(552)  Cabinet maker
(553)  Chair maker
(554)  Cradle maker
(555)  Turner
(559)  Wooden plough maker
(561)  Baker
(562)  Butcher
(563)  Beer maker, brewer
(564)  Tobaconist
(571)  Wagon builder
(572)  Wheelwright
(573)  Carriage maker
(574)  Carriage smith
(575)  Carriage trimmer
(576)  Carriage painter
(577)  Coach maker
```

```
(581) Carpenter
(582) Painter
(583) Bricklayer, mason
(584) Brick maker
(585) Stone mason
(586) Wall layer
(587) Paper hanger
(591) Quarryman
(592) Stone cutter
(593) Sculptor
(594) Machinist
(595) Mechanic
(596) Moulder
(597) Pump maker
(598) Millwright
(622) Tanner
(623) Bark grinder
(631) Loom operator
(632) Wool carder
(633) Cotton factory, unspecified
(634) Weaver
(635) Cotton dresser
(642) Foundry man
(643) Furnace hand
(711) Housekeeper, domestic
(712) Servant
(721) Janitor
(722) Enlisted soldier
(730) Laundress
(740) Maid
(741) Kitchen maid
(742) Waiting maids
(750) Watchman
(760) Laborers in hotel, restaurant
(761) Osteler, stableman
(762) Bartender
(771) Stage driver
(772) Teamster
(773) Steamboat pilot
(774) Gate tender
(775) Seaman
(776) Boatman
(777) Cartman
(830) Farm laborer
(831) Dairy work
(832) Drover
(850) Wood cutter
(870) Railroad laborer
(890) Day laborer
(891) Ditcher
```

```
                   (909) Illegible
                   (910) Gentleman, lady
                   (920) Retired
                   (931) Tinkerer
                   (932) Root digging
                   (934) Travling
                   (940) Student
                   (941) Student of law
                   (942) Student of medicine
                   (950) Apprentice
                   (959) Apprentice to machinist
                   (990) Unemployed
                   (991) Retired
                   (000)NO OCCUPATION GIVEN
1      36          LNDOWN,
                   Landowner in 1855
                   (0) no
                   (1) yes
1      37          LITRCY,
                   Literate
                   (0) yes, age 16+ can read and write
                   (1) can't read
                   (2) can't write
                   (3) can neither read nor write
                   (4) illegible
                   (5) idiot
1      39          NATIVE,
                   National origin or subdivision thereof
                   (1) Town of enumeration
                   (2) Elsewhere in Schoharie County
                   (3) Elsewhere in New York
                   (4) Elsewhere in the United States
                   (5) German born
                   (6) Irish born
                   (7) English, Welsh, or Scottish
                   (8) Canada or elsewhere in Europe
1      40-45       POB,
                   Place of birth
                   see part 2: Places
1      47-48       SPSAGE,
                   Age of spouse in 1855
1      49-54       SPSPOB,
                   Birthplace of spouse
                   see part 2: Places
1      59-64       PRRZ1,
                   First prior place of residence
                   see part 2: Places
```

CARD NO.	COLUMN NO.	VARIABLE NAME
1	66-71	PRRZ2, Second prior place of residence see part 2: Places
1	73-80	PRRZ3, Third prior place of residence see part 2: Places
2	1	CNUM2, Card 2 of 5
2	3-8	CASEID2, Six digit number unique to this case
2	10-11	YR55, 55 - Census year of data on cards 1,2,3
2	12-17	RZ55, Place of residence in 1855 see part 2: Places
2	21-24	DWLNM55, Dwelling numbered in order of visitation
2	26	DWLMAT, Material used in construction of dwelling (0) unknown (1) log (2) plank-board (3) frame (4) brick (5) stone (6) slabs (7) block (9) missing data
2	27-30	DWLVAL, Dwelling value in whole dollars (-9) missing value
2	33	DLFMZ55, Number of co-residing family groups
2	34-35	DLPRZ55, Number of co-residng people
2	37-40	FAMNM55, Each family in order of visitation
2	41-42	FMSIZ55, Persons in this family group
2	43-44	FMRLZ55, Co-residing family members relate to head
2	45-46	RLPRZ55, Co-residents related to this person
2	47-48	NNRLZ, Co-residents not related to this person

CARD NO.	COLUMN NO.	VARIABLE NAME
2	50-52	FMTYP55, Type of family group (100) Everyone is related (110) Single person family (120) Married couple without children (121) Married couple with children (130) Denuded family -head is widowed- (140) Extended family (150) Parentless related "children" (200) Augmented family (210) Includes boarders-lodgers (220) Includes servants-employees (230) Combination of 210 & 220 (300) Both extended and augmented (400) Hotels-inns-boarding houses (500) Jail, asylum (600) Seminary-academy-boarding school (700) County poorhouse

CARD NO.	COLUMN NO.	VARIABLE NAME
2	53	CHU5, Children of this person aged 0-4 in 1855
2	54	CH59, Children of this person aged 5-9 in 1855
2	55	CH1014, Children of this person aged 10-14 in 1855
2	56	CH1519, Children of this person aged 15-19 in 1855
2	57	CH2024, Children of this person aged 20-24 in 1855
2	58	CH2529, Children of this person aged 25-29 in 1855
2	59-60	CHTOTL, Total number of children in 1855
2	62-63	KNNM55, People with this surname in this town
2	64-65	KNHD55, Family heads with this surname in this town
3	1	CNUM3, Card 3 of 5
3	3-8	CASEID3, Six digit number unique to this case
3	10-17	IMPACR, Improved farm acreage (-9) missing value

```
CARD   COLUMN   VARIABLE
NO.    NO.      NAME

 3     18-25    NOIMPR,
                Unimproved farm acreage
                (-9)missing value
 3     26-31    FRMVAL,
                Total value of this farm land in dollars
                (-9)missing value
 3     32-36    STKVAL,
                Value of livestock in dollars
                (-9)missing value
 3     37-41    TOOLS,
                Value of agricultural implements
                (-9)missing value
 3     42-50    TOTACS,
                Total acreage of this farm
                (-9)missing value
 3     53-58    PCTIMP,
                Percentage of farm improved
                (-9)missing value
 3     59-64    TOTVAL,
                Total value of land, stock, and tools
                (-9)missing value
 3     66-72    VALPRAC,
                Value per acre of farm land
                (-9)missing value
 4      1       CNUM4,
                Card 4 of 5
 4      3-8     CASEID1,
                Six digit number unique to this case
 4      10      STATUS,
                Persister or non-persister
                (1)persister, found in 1860
                (2)migrant, found in 1860
                (3)persister, found in 1865
                (4)migrant, found in 1865
                (5)persister missed by census
                (6)assumed migrant
                (7)deceased probably in situ
                (8)deceased after migrating
                (9)unknown
```

```
CARD    COLUMN   VARIABLE
NO.     NO.      NAME

 4      11-12    CNDTN,
                 Source of data for determination of status
                 (00) Not found in 1860 census manuscript
                 (11) Found with certainty in 1860 census
                 (12) Probably is person in 1860 census
                 (13) Might be person in 1860 census
                 (21) Found in 1865 census
                 (22) Might be person in 1865 census
                 (24) Found in 65 census - migrated 55 to65
                 (31) Located in church records
                 (41) Married and found in census
                 (50) Married and not found in census
                 (61) Found using Albany city directory
                 (62) Possibly found using Albany directory
                 (63) May be person in Albany directory
                 (71) Found using reference in newspaper
                 (91) Dead obit or cemetary inscription
                 (92) Dead, spouse is widow in 1860
                 (99) Died after migrating
 4      14-15    YR60,
                 60, census year of data for card 4
 4      16-21    LOC60,
                 Place of residence in 1860
                 see part 2: Places
 4      28-35    DIST,
                 Distance between 1855 and 1860 places
                 of residence measured in straight line
                 between town centroids
 4      37-38    AGE60,
                 Age in 1860
 4      39-40    REL60,
                 Assumed relation to household head in 1860
 4      41-43    OCC60,
                 Occupation in 1860
                 see codes above, OCC55
 4      44       NEWFAM
                 Family formed between 1855 and 1860
                 (0)no
                 (1)yes
 4      45-46    KIN60,
                 Same surnamed persons persisting
                 in 1855 place of residence
 4      48-50    FMTYP60,
                 Household type in 1860
                 see codes above, FMTYP55
```

CARD NO.	COLUMN NO.	VARIABLE NAME
4	51-52	FMPRS60, Co-residents in this family group
4	53-54	FMRLS60, Co-residents related to head
4	55-56	RLPRS60, Co-residents related to this case
4	57	CLU5, Children of this person aged 0-4 in 1860
4	58	CL59, Children, aged 5-9 years in 1860
4	59	CL1017, Children, aged 10-17 years in 1860
4	61-63	HDOC60, Occupation of household head in 1860 see codes above, OCC55
4	65-69	HDRLP60, Value of real estate owned by head in 1860
4	70-74	HDPRP60, Value of personal estate owned by head, ´60
5	1	CNUM5, Card 5 of 5
5	3-8	CASEID5, Six digit number unique to this case
5	10-11	YR65, 65, year for data on card 5
5	12-17	LOC65, Place of residence in 1865 see part 2: Places (-9) missing data

Part 2: Places


```
(00)UNKNOWN
(01)UNITED STATES
   (01)ALABAMA
   (02)ALASKA
   (03)ARIZONA
   (04)ARKANSAS
   (05)CALIFORNIA
      (01)STANISLAUS COUNTY
         (01)LAGRANGE
   (06)COLORADO
   (07)CONNECTICUT
   (08)DELAWARE
   (09)FLORIDA
   (10)GEORGIA
   (11)HAWAII
   (12)IDAHO
   (13)ILLINOIS
      (01)COOK COUNTY
         (01)CHICAGO
         (02)LYDEN CENTER
      (02)KANKAKEE COUNTY
         (02)KANKAKEE CITY
      (03)LOGAN COUNTY
         (01)LINCOLN
      (04)PEORIA COUNTY
         (01)PEORIA
      (06)LASALLE COUNTY
         (01)MENDOTA TWP
            (01)MENDOTA CITY
      (07)JO DAVIESS COUNTY
         (01)HANOVER
   (14)INDIANA
   (15)IOWA
      (01)DELAWARE COUNTY
         (01)SOUTH FORK TOWNSHIP
   (16)KANSAS
   (17)KENTUCKY
   (18)LOUISIANA
   (19)MAINE
   (20)MARYLAND
   (21)MASSACHUSETTS
      (01)BOSTON
      (02)WORCHESTER
   (22)MICHIGAN
      (01)WAYNE COUNTY
         (01)DETRIOT
```

(23)MINNESOTA
(24)MISSISSIPPI
(25)MISSOURI
(26)MONTANA
(27)NEBRASKA
(30)NEW JERSEY
   (01)ESSEX COUNTY
      (01)NEW BRUNSWICK
      (02)ORANGE
(31)NEW MEXICO
(32)NEW YORK
   (01)ALBANY
      (01)BERNE
      (02)BETHLEHEM
      (03)COEYMANS
      (04)GUILDERLAND
         (01)HAMILTONVILLE
      (05)KNOX
      (06)NEW SCOTLAND
      (07)RENSSELAERVILLE
      (08)WESTERLO
      (10)ALBANY CITY
         (09)WARD 9
         (10)WARD 10
   (02)ALLEGANY
   (03)BROOME
      (01)SANDFORD
         (01)DEPOSIT
      (02)WINDSOR
      (03)CHENANGO
      (04)BARKER
      (05)UNION
      (06)COLESVILLE
      (07)PORT CRANE
   (04)CATTARAUGUS
   (05)CAYUGA
      (01)AUBURN CITY
   (06)CHAUTAUQUA
   (07)CHEMUNG
   (08)CHENANGO
      (01)NEW BERLIN
      (02)AFTON
   (09)CLINTON
   (10)COLUMBIA
      (01)CLERMONT

```
(11)CORTLAND
    (01)HOMER
    (02)MARATHON
    (03)CORTLANDVILLE
    (04)PREBLE
(12)DELAWARE
    (01)ROXBURY
    (02)HARPERSFIELD
    (03)DELHI
    (04)COLCHESTER
    (05)KORTRIGHT
    (06)ANDES
    (07)HAMDEN
    (08)MIDDLETOWN
    (09)STAMFORD
    (10)DAVENPORT
    (11)TOMPKINS
    (12)SIDNEY
    (13)HANCOCK
    (14)WALTON
(13)DUTCHESS
    (01)POUGHKEEPSIE
    (02)PLEASANT VALLEY
(14)ERIE
(15)ESSEX
(16)FRANKLIN
(17)FULTON
    (01)STRATFORD
(18)GENESEE
(19)GREENE
    (01)PRATTSVILLE
    (02)NEW BALTIMORE
    (03)GREENEVILLE
    (04)COXSACKIE
    (05)DURHAM
    (06)ASHLAND
    (07)CATSKILL
    (08)WINDHAM
    (09)CAIRO
    (10)LEXINGTON
(20)HAMILTON
(21)HERKIMER
    (01)LITCHFIELD
(22)JEFFERSON
    (01)CARTHAGE
    (02)WATERTOWN
(23)KINGS
(24)LEWIS
```

(25) LIVINGSTON
(26) MADISON
(27) MONROE
(28) MONTGOMERY
   (01) AMSTERDAM
   (02) ROOT
   (03) CANAJOHARIE
   (04) FLORIDA
   (05) CHARLESTON
   (06) GLEN
      (01) FONDA
(29) NEW YORK
(30) NIAGRA
(31) ONEIDA
   (01) CAMDEN
(32) ONONDAGA
   (01) CLAY
(33) ONTARIO
(34) ORANGE
(35) ORLEANS
   (01) SHELBY
(36) OSWEGO
   (10) OSWEGO CITY
(37) OTSEGO
   (01) CHERRY VALLEY
   (02) DECATUR
   (03) WORCESTER
   (04) WESTFORD
   (05) MILFORD
   (06) UNADILLA
   (07) MARYLAND
   (08) LAURENS
   (09) ONEONTA
   (10) ROSEBOOM
(38) PUTNAM
(39) QUEENS
(40) RENSSELAER
   (01) TROY
   (02) SCHODACK
(41) RICHMOND
(42) ROCKLAND
(43) ST. LAWRENCE
(44) SARATOGA
   (01) CHARLTON
   (02) BALLSTON
   (03) HALF MOON
   (04) MILTON
   (05) STILLWATER

```
(45) SCHENECTADY
     (01) DUANESBURGH
     (02) ROTTERDAM
     (03) NISKAYMA
     (04) SCHENECTADY CITY
          (00) WARD NUMBER
     (05) GLENVILLE
     (06) PRINCETON
(46) SCHOHARIE
     (01) BLENHEIM
          (X ) ENUMERATION DISTRICT NUMBER
          ( 0) FARM
          ( 2) NORTH BLENHEIM-PATCHIN HOLLOW
          ( 3) EMMINENCE
          ( 9) UNDETERMINED
     (02) BROOME
     (03) CARLISLE  .
     (04) COBLESKILL
     (05) CONESVILLE
     (06) ESPERANCE
          (X ) ENUMERATION DISTRICT NUMBER
          ( 0) FARM
          ( 1) ESPERANCE
          ( 2) SLOANSVILE
          ( 9) UNDETERMINED
     (07) FULTON
     (08) GILBOA
          (X ) ENUMERATION DISTRICT NUMBER
          ( 0) FARM
          ( 1) GILBOA
          ( 2) BROOME CENTER
          ( 3) MACKEY CORNER
          ( 4) SOUTH GILBOA
          ( 5) WEST GILBOA
     (09) JEFFERSON
     (10) MIDDLEBURGH
     (11) RICHMONDVILLE
          (X ) ENUMERATION DISTRICT NUMBER
          ( 0) FARM
          ( 1) RICHMONDVILLE
          ( 2) WARNERVILLE
     (12) SCHOHARIE
          (X ) ENUMERATION DISTRICT NUMBER
          ( 0) FARM
          ( 1) CENTRAL BRIDGE
          ( 2) SCHOHARIE
          ( 3) BLACK DISTRICT OF SCHOHARIE
          ( 4) OLD FORT
```

```
        (13) SEWARD
        (14) SHARON
        (15) SUMMIT
        (16) WRIGHT
            (X ) ENUMERATION DISTRICT NUMBER
            ( 0) FARM
            ( 1) GALLUPVILLE
    (47) SCHUYLER
    (48) SENECA
    (49) STEUBEN
    (50) SUFFOLK
    (51) SULLIVAN
    (52) TIOGA
        (01) OWEGO
    (53) TOMPKINS
    (54) ULSTER
        (01) WOODSTOCK
    (55) WARREN
    (56) WASHINGTON
        (01) CAMBRIDGE
    (57) WAYNE
    (58) WESTCHESTER
    (59) WYOMING
    (60) YATES
(33) NORTH CAROLINA
(34) NORTH DAKOTA
(35) OHIO
(36) OKLAHOMA
(37) OREGON
(38) PENNSYLVANIA
    (02) WESTCHESTER
(39) RHODE ISLAND
(40) SOUTH CAROLINA
(41) SOUTH DAKOTA
(42) TENNESSEE
(43) TEXAS
(44) UTAH
(45) VERMONT
    (01) WINDHAM
(46) VIRGINIA
(47) WASHINGTON STATE
(48) WEST VIRGINIA
(49) WISCONSIN
    (01) WALWORTH COUNTY
        (01) DELEVAN
        (02) DARIEN
        (03) WALWORTH
```

```
        (02)WAUPACA  COUNTY
            (01)WEYAUWEGA
        (03)RACINE  COUNTY
            (01)RAYMOND
        (04)LACROSSE  COUNTY
            (01)BARRE
        (05)WAUKESHA  COUNTY
            (01)SUMMITT
            (02)MUKERNANGO
        (06)MONROE  COUNTY
            (01)PORTLAND
        (07)ROCK  COUNTY
            (01)HARMONY
        (08)FOND  DU  LAC  COUNTY
            (01)RIPON
    (50)WYOMING
    (51)WASHINGTON-DISTRICT  OF  COLUMBIA
(02)GERMANY
    (01)BERLIN
(03)ENGLAND
(04)SCOTLAND
(05)IRELAND
    (01)ULSTER
(06)WALES
(07)FRANCE
(08)CANADA
    (01)QUEBEC,  LOWER  CANADA
        (01)MONTREAL
    (02)NOVA  SCOTIA
    (03)ONTARIO,  UPPER  CANADA
(09)DENMARK
(10)GREECE
(11)SWEDEN
(12)PRUSSIA
(13)HOLLAND
(14)POLAND
(15)HUNGARY
(16)SWITZERLAND
    (01)BERN
(17)BELGIUM
```

APPENDIX D

FIVE-YEAR MORTALITY ESTIMATES FOR THE INITIAL SAMPLE (1)

Town of Blenheim

Age	Males	Est. Deaths	Females	Est. Deaths
0-1	33	4.60	15	1.77
1-4	87	6.16	92	6.60
5-9	74	1.52	88	1.88
10-14	85	1.27	82	1.36
15-19	74	1.62	74	1.67
20-24	53	1.65	54	1.56
25-29	51	1.74	51	1.67
30-34	52	2.03	48	1.78
35-39	38	1.76	35	1.45
40-44	38	2.19	28	1.30
45-49	20	1.42	21	1.13
50-54	23	2.17	25	1.79
55-59	23	2.87	16	1.52
60-64	15	2.62	15	2.10
65-69	6	1.44	10	1.97
70-74	6	2.01	5	1.46
75-79	3	1.39	3	1.25
80+	3	3.00	2	2.00
	684	41.55	664	34.26

Death Rate = 56.20

Est. Survivors =
   1348 (684 + 664) - 76 (41.55 + 34.26) = 1272

1. Calculated from Level 13 West, Coale and Demeny (1966).

Source: Manuscript Census of 1855

Town of Esperance

Age	Males	Est. Deaths	Females	Est. Deaths
0-1	18	2.51	19	2.25
1-4	54	3.83	59	4.22
5-9	83	1.71	89	1.90
10-14	78	1.16	93	1.54
15-19	69	1.51	72	1.63
20-24	48	1.49	63	1.82
25-29	36	1.23	63	2.06
30-34	44	1.72	49	1.81
35-39	48	2.22	55	2.28
40-44	49	2.82	39	1.81
45-49	32	2.28	28	1.51
50-54	18	1.70	19	1.36
55-59	19	2.37	20	1.91
60-64	19	3.32	20	2.80
65-69	14	3.37	21	4.16
70-74	8	2.69	8	2.33
75-79	3	1.39	3	1.25
80+	3	3.00	7	7.00
	643	40.32	727	43.64

Death Rate = 61.30

Est. Survivors =
   1370 (643 + 727) - 84 (40.32 + 43.64) = 1286

Town of Gilboa

Age	Males	Est. Deaths	Females	Est. Deaths
0-1	27	3.76	39	4.61
1-4	165	11.69	149	1.07
5-9	171	3.52	184	3.93
10-14	163	2.43	207	3.43
15-19	146	3.20	126	2.85
20-24	105	3.27	123	3.55
25-29	85	2.90	87	2.84
30-34	81	3.17	74	2.74
35-39	73	3.39	64	2.66
40-44	65	3.74	68	3.16
45-49	59	4.20	64	3.44
50-54	53	5.00	42	3.01
55-59	21	2.62	36	3.43
60-64	37	6.47	30	4.20
65-69	24	5.78	25	4.95
70-74	20	6.71	17	4.96
75-79	9	4.18	9	3.75
80+	5	5.00	5	5.00
	1309	81.03	1349	63.58

Death Rate = 54.40

Est. Survivors =
  2658 (1309 + 1349) − 145 (81.03 + 63.58) = 2513

Town of Richmondville

Age	Males	Est. Deaths	Females	Est. Deaths
0-1	27	3.76	18	2.13
1-4	112	7.93	115	8.24
5-9	147	3.03	126	2.69
10-14	122	1.82	124	2.06
15-19	99	2.17	111	2.51
20-24	88	2.74	86	2.48
25-29	87	2.97	72	2.35
30-34	79	3.09	81	3.00
35-39	67	3.11	61	2.53
40-44	36	2.07	43	2.00
45-49	35	2.49	34	1.83
50-54	39	3.68	33	2.37
55-59	26	3.24	32	3.05
60-64	21	3.67	23	3.22
65-69	16	3.85	15	2.97
70-74	11	3.69	12	3.50
75-79	14	6.50	6	2.50
80+	2	2.00	7	7.00
	1028	65.62	999	56.43

Death Rate = 60.20

Est. Survivors =
  2027 (1028 + 999) − 122 (65.62 + 56.43) = 1905

Town of Schoharie

Age	Males	Est. Deaths	Females	Est. Deaths
0-1	45	6.27	33	3.91
1-4	169	11.97	146	10.47
5-9	182	3.75	173	3.70
10-14	147	2.19	187	3.10
15-19	158	3.46	165	3.73
20-24	128	3.98	147	4.24
25-29	111	3.79	130	4.25
30-34	99	3.87	83	3.10
35-39	81	3.76	85	3.53
40-44	70	4.03	77	3.58
45-49	56	3.99	49	2.63
50-54	56	5.29	52	3.73
55-59	32	3.99	35	3.33
60-64	33	5.77	36	5.04
65-69	17	4.09	21	4.16
70-74	19	6.38	18	5.25
75-79	7	^.25	7	2.91
80+	7	7.00	7	7.00
	1417	86.83	1451	77.66

Death Rate = 57.40

Est. Survivors =
2868 (1417 + 1451) - 164 (86.83 + 77.66) = 2704

Town of Wright

| | | Est. | | Est. |
Age	Males	Deaths	Females	Deaths
0-1	15	2.09	21	2.48
1-4	112	7.93	87	6.24
5-9	101	2.08	105	2.24
10-14	107	1.60	104	1.73
15-19	90	1.97	78	1.76
20-24	66	2.05	75	2.16
25-29	59	2.01	64	2.09
30-34	55	2.15	54	2.00
35-39	47	2.18	48	1.99
40-44	44	2.53	40	1,86
45-49	31	2.21	32	1.72
50-54	28	2.64	25	1.79
55-59	18	2.24	19	1.81
60-64	21	3.67	19	2.66
65-69	21	5.06	14	2.77
70-74	9	3.02	10	2.92
75-79	8	3.72	12	5.00
80+	7	7.00	5	5.00
	839	56.15	812	48.22

Death Rate = 63.20

Est. Survivors =
  1651 (839 + 812) - 104 (56.15 + 48.22) = 1547

APPENDIX E

MOBILITY AND MORTALITY OF MALE HEADS OF FAMILIES, BY TOWN, 1855-1860

Town of Blenheim

				1860			1865		
Age	N	Est. Dead(1)	Known Dead(2)	Non-Mig.	Mig.	Unkn.(3)	Non-Mig.	Mig.	Unkn.(4)
15-19	0	0.00	0	0	0	0	0	0	0
20-24	13	0.40(0)	0	7	1	5	–	3	2
25-29	33	1.16(1)	0	24	7	2	1	1	0
30-34	47	1.84(2)	0	30	13	2	1	1	0
35-39	30	1.39(1)	1	19	6	4	–	1	3
40-44	32	1.84(2)	2	22	6	2	–	1	1
45-49	17	1.21(1)	0	12	3	1	–	–	1
50-54	21	1.98(2)	2	14	4	1	–	1	0
55-59	21	2.62(3)	1	18	0	0	1	–	0
60-64	12	2.10(2)	1	8	1	1	1	–	0
65-69	4	.96(1)	2	2	0	0	–	–	0
70-74	5	1.68(2)	2	3	0	0	–	–	0
75-79	2	.93(1)	2	0	0	0	–	–	0
80+	1	1.00(1)	0	1	0	0	–	–	0
	---	----	--	--	--	--	--	--	--
	239	19.11(19)	13	159	41	18	4	8	7
	---	----	--	--	--	--	--	--	--

1 Estimated from Level 13 West, Coale and Demeny (1960).
2 Compiled from cemetary records, obituaries, and census comparison.
3 N minus non-migrants, migrants, and either estimated deaths or known
   deaths which ever is greater without generating a negative number.
4 Not adjusted for mortality between 1860 and 1865.

Town of Esperance

Age	N	Est. Dead(1)	Known Dead(2)	1860			1865		
				Non-Mig.	Mig.	Unkn.(3)	Non-Mig.	Mig.	Unkn.(4)
15-19	0	0.00	0	0	0	0	0	0	0
20-24	6	.19(0)	1	1	2	2	-	-	2
25-29	20	.68(1)	1	11	6	2	1	-	1
30-34	34	1.33(1)	1	19	5	9	-	2	7
35-39	42	1.95(2)	4	30	1	7	2	2	3
40-44	43	2.47(3)	0	27	10	3	2	1	0
45-49	30	2.14(2)	0	25	4	0	-	-	0
50-54	17	1.60(2)	1	14	1	0	-	-	0
55-59	17	2.12(2)	2	14	1	0	-	-	0
60-64	13	2.27(2)	1	11	1	0	-	-	0
65-69	11	2.65(3)	3	8	0	0	-	-	0
70-74	4	1.34(1)	1	3	0	0	-	1	0
75-79	2	.93(1)	0	1	0	1	-	1	0
80+	3	3.00(3)	3	0	0	1	-	-	0
	242	22.67(23)	18	164	31	24	5	6	13

Town of Gilboa

				1860				1865		
Age	N	Est. Dead(1)	Known Dead(2)	Non-Mig.	Mig.	Unkn.(3)		Non-Mig.	Mig.	Unkn.(4)
15-19	1	0.02(0)	0	1	0	0		0	0	0
20-24	21	.65(1)	0	11	6	3		1	1	1
25-29	63	2.15(2)	1	30	15	16		2	2	12
30-34	71	2.78(3)	3	39	16	13		2	2	9
35-39	66	3.07(3)	4	38	15	9		—	—	9
40-44	58	3.34(3)	2	39	18	8		2	—	6
45-49	54	3.85(4)	1	43	5	2		1	—	1
50-54	47	4.44(4)	0	41	3	0		1	—	0
55-59	21	2.62(3)	2	17	1	0		—	—	0
60-64	35	6.12(6)	4	29	2	0		—	—	0
65-69	22	5.30(5)	7	12	0	3		—	—	2
70-74	16	5.37(5)	4	10	1	1		—	1	0
75-79	5	2.32(3)	1	4	0	0		—	—	0
80+	2	2.00(2)	1	1	0	0		—	—	0
	482	44.03(44)	30	315	72	55		9	7	40

Town of Richmondville

Age	N	Est. Dead(1)	Known Dead(2)	1860			1865		
				Non-Mig.	Mig.	Unkn.(3)	Non-Mig.	Mig.	Unkn.(4)
15-19	0	0.00	0	1	0	0	0	0	0
20-24	20	.62(1)	0	13	4	2	-	1	1
25-29	56	1.91(2)	1	35	13	6	2	4	0
30-34	59	2.31(2)	1	36	15	6	-	1	5
35-39	64	2.97(3)	0	45	9	7	-	2	5
40-44	35	2.01(2)	2	24	6	3	-	1	3
45-49	32	2.28(2)	5	20	4	3	-	1	2
50-54	37	3.49(3)	2	29	4	1	-	-	1
55-59	22	2.74(3)	2	18	2	0	-	-	0
60-64	17	2.97(3)	3	12	2	0	-	-	0
65-69	12	2.89(3)	2	9	1	0	-	-	0
70-74	5	1.68(2)	1	4	0	0	-	-	0
5-79	8	3.72(4)	0	7	1	0	-	-	0
80+	0	0.00	0	0	0	0	-	-	0
	367	29.59 (30)	18	252	61	28	2	9	17

Town of Schoharie

Age	N	Est. Dead(1)	1860				1865		
			Known Dead(2)	Non-Mig.	Mig.	Unkn.(3)	Non-Mig.	Mig.	Unkn.(4)
15-19	1	0.02(0)	0	1	0	0	0	0	0
20-24	22	.68(1)	1	13	1	7	–	1	7
25-29	57	1.94(2)	2	33	13	9	5	1	3
30-34	71	2.78(3)	2	44	16	8	2	2	4
35-39	69	3.20(3)	1	49	15	8	–	1	7
40-44	60	3.45(3)	1	41	9	1	1	–	0
45-49	53	3.77(4)	2	42	5	2	1	1	0
50-54	51	4.81(5)	4	41	2	3	2	1	0
55-59	26	3.24(3)	4	20	1	1	1	–	0
60-64	27	4.72(5)	4	21	2	0	–	1	0
65-69	13	3.13(3)	4	8	0	1	–	–	0
70-74	17	5.71(6)	2	15	0	0	–	–	0
75-79	5	2.32(2)	2	3	0	0	–	–	0
80+	2	2.00(2)	1	1	0	0	–	–	0
	474	39.45(42)	30	330	64	42	12	7	23

Town of Wright

Age	N	Est. Dead(1)	1860				1865		
			Known Dead(2)	Non-Mig.	Mig.	Unkn.(3)	Non-Mig.	Mig.	Unkn.(4)
15-19	1	0.00	0	0	0	0	0	0	0
20-24	7	.22(0)	0	3	2	2	-	-	2
25-29	35	1.38(1)	1	22	8	4	1	-	3
30-34	45	2.09(2)	0	30	12	1	1	-	0
35-39	41	1.90(2)	0	28	6	5	1	-	4
40-44	41	2.36(2)	2	29	8	2	-	-	2
45-49	27	1.92(2)	1	19	6	0	-	-	0
50-54	24	2.27(2)	2	17	2	3	-	-	0
55-59	17	2.12(2)	1	11	4	1	-	1	0
60-64	17	2.97(3)	3	14	0	0	-	-	0
65-69	16	3.85(4)	4	11	1	0	-	-	0
70-74	7	2.35(2)	3	3	0	1	1	-	0
75-79	5	2.32(2)	1	3	1	0	-	-	0
80+	3	3.00	1	2	0	0	-	-	0
	285	28.75(27)	19	192	50	19	4	1	11

APPENDIX F

Occupational Classification

Group 1: Learned professions

(161) BANKER
(131) CIVIL ENGINEER
(150) CLERGY
(151) CLERGYMAN
(274) COLLEGE TEACHER
(122) DENTIST
(123) DOCTOR
(132) GEOLOGIST
(910) GENTLEMAN, LADY
(125) HOMEOPATHIC PHYSICIAN
(273) INSTRUCTOR IN PRIVATE SCHOOL OR ACADEMY
(241) JUDGE,JUSTICE OF THE PEACE
(111) LAWYER
(152) MINISTER
(126) NURSE
(121) PHYSICIAN
(124) PHYSICIAN & SURGEON
(271) PRINCIPAL OF PRIVATE SCHOOL
(134) RAILROAD CONTRACTOR
(153) REVEREND DOCTOR
(279) SCHOOL ADMINISTRATOR
(773) STEAMBOAT PILOT
(272) STEWARD OF PRIVATE SCHOOL
(133) SURVEYOR

Group 2: Business and civil service

(431) BANK CLERK
(420) BOOKKEEPER, ACCOUNTANT
(430) CLERK
(246) CONSTABLES
(233) DEALER
(231) DEALER IN PATENT WRIGHT
(213) CLOTHIER
(441) COTTON MILL AGENT
(215) DRUGGIST
(471) EXPRESSMAN
(211) GENERAL MERCHANDISER
(219) GRAIN DEALER
(216) GROCER
(214) HARDWARE DEALER
(472) MAIL CARRIER
(242) MAIL CONTRACTOR

```
(221) MANUFACTURER OF AGRICULTURAL IMPLEMENTS
(222) MANUFACTURER OF LEATHER GOODS
(223) MANUFACTURER OF CLOTHING
(225) MANUFACTURER OF WAGONS
(227) MANUFACTURER OF CARRIAGES
(228) MANUFACTURER OF SASH AND BLINDS
(255) MARBLE DEALER
(210) MERCHANT
(432) MERCHANT´S CLERK
(253) MILLER
(252) NURSERYMAN
(413) PEDDLAR
(248) POORHOUSE KEEPER
(410) SALES
(260) SELLER OF FOOD AND LODGING
(243) SHERIFF
(230) SMALL FINANCE, REAL ESTATE, & INSURANCE
(232) SPECULATOR
(256) STAGE PROPRIETOR
(244) TEACHERS OTHER THAN COLLEGE
(414) TIN PEDDLAR
(412) TRAVELING MERCHANT
(247) FIREMAN
(249) INSPECTOR OF PUBLIC WORKS
(261) RESTAURANTER
(262) ROOMING HOUSE
(263) HOTEL OPERATOR
(264) INNKEEPER
(266) BEER PEDDLAR
(275) SCHOOL TEACHER
(276) MUSIC TEACHER
(277) WRITING TEACHER
(278) ORNAMENTAL TEACHER
(299) FANNING MILL MAKER
```

Group 3: Craftsmen.

```
(351) SAWYER
(352) LUMBERMAN
(353) LUMBERING
(251) BARBER
(267) SEGAR -CIGAR- MAKER
(959) APPRENTICE TO MACHINIST
(931) TINKERER
(360) AGRIULTURE L-S IL-T ERATURST
(511) JEWELER
(512) WATCHMAKER
(513) PRINTER
(514) CLOCKMAKER
(515) GUNSMITH
```

(516) PAPER MAKING
(517) SILVERSMITH
(518) ENGRAVER
(519) DEGAR ARTIST -DEUGAROTYPES-
(521) SHOEMAKER
(522) TANNERY FOREMAN
(524) CORDWAIN
(527) HARNESS MAKER
(531) TAILOR
(532) DRESSMAKER
(533) SEAMSTRESS
(534) HATTER
(535) MILLENER -LADY'S HATS-
(536) WEAVER
(537) MILLENER & DRESSMAKER
(541) TINSMITH
(542) BLACKSMITH
(543) SILVERPLATER
(544) SILVER BURNISHER
(545) TINNER
(546) SILVERSMITH
(547) TINMAN
(548) PILL BOX MAKER
(551) COOPER
(552) CABINET MAKER
(553) CHAIR MAKER
(554) CRADLE MAKER
(555) TURNER
(559) WOODEN PLOUGH MAKER
(561) BAKER
(562) BUTCHER
(563) BEER MAKER, BREWER
(564) TOBACONIST
(571) WAGON BUILDER
(572) WHEELWRIGHT
(573) CARRIAGE MAKER
(574) CARRIAGE SMITH
(575) CARRIAGE TRIMMER
(576) CARRIAGE PAINTER
(577) COACH MAKER
(581) CARPENTER
(582) PAINTER
(583) BRICKLAYER,MASON
(584) BRICK MAKER
(585) STONE MASON
(586) WALL LAYER
(587) PAPER HANGER
(591) QUARRYMAN
(592) STONE CUTTER
(593) SCULPTOR

           (594) MACHINIST
           (595) MECHANIC
           (596) MOULDER
           (597) PUMP MAKER
           (598) MILLWRIGHT
           (622) TANNER

Group 4: Agriculture.

           (310) FARMER WHO OWNS LAND
           (320) FARMER WITHOUT LAND
           (330) BEE KEEPER

Group 5: Semi-skilled workers, service wrokers, laborers

           (623) BARK GRINDER
           (631) LOOM OPERATOR
           (632) WOOL CARDER
           (633) COTTON FACTORY, UNSPECIFIED
           (634) WEAVER
           (635) COTTON DRESSER
           (642) FOUNDRY MAN
           (643) FURNACE HAND
           (711) HOUSEKEEPER, DOMESTIC
           (712) SERVANT
           (721) JANITOR
           (722) ENLISTED SOLDIER
           (730) LAUNDRESS
           (740) MAID
           (741) KITCHEN MAID
           (742) WAITING MAID
           (750) WATCHMAN
           (761) OSTELER, STABLEMAN
           (762) BARTENDER
           (771) STAGE DRIVER
           (772) TEAMSTER
           (774) GATE TENDER
           (775) SEAMAN
           (776) BOATMAN
           (777) CARTMAN
           (830) FARM LABORER
           (831) DAIRY WORK
           (832) DROVER
           (850) WOOD CUTTER
           (870) RAILROAD LABORER
           (890) DAY LABORER
           (891) DITCHER
           (930) MISCELLANEOUS
           (932) ROOT DIGGING

BIBLIOGRAPHY

Akerman, Sune, Bo Kronborg, and Thomas Nilsson. (1977) "Emigration, Family and Kinship," American Studies in Scandinavia, 9:105-122.

(The) Albany Directory for 1860. Albany, New York: Adams, Sampson, and Co.

Alcorn, Richard S. (1974) "Leadership and Stability in Mid Nineteenth Century America: A Case Study of an Illinois Town," Journal of American History, 61:685-702.

Allen, James P. (1977) "Changes in the American Propensity to Migrate", Annals of the Association of American Geographers, 67:577-587.

Anderson, Michael. (1971) Family Structure in Nineteenth Century Lancashire. Cambridge: Cambridge University Press.

Anderson, Russell H. (1925) "Agriculture in New York, 1830-1850." Unpublished M. A. Thesis in History, University of Illinois, Urbana.

Barber, Gertrude. (1936) "Cemetery Records of Schoharie County to 1932." Unpublished typescript at Schoharie County Historical Society Library, Old Stone Fort Museum, Schoharie, New York.

Barron, Harold Seth. (1980) "Their Town: Economy and Society in a Settled Rural Community; Chelsea, Vermont, 1840-1900." Unpublished Ph. D. Thesis in History, University of Pennsylvania.

Barrows, Robert G. (1981) "Hurryin´ Hoosiers and the American ´Pattern´: Geographic Mobility in Indianapolis and Urban North America," Social Science History, 5:197-222.

Bash, Wendell H. (1963) "Changing Birth Rates in Developing America: New York State, 1840-1875," Milbank Memorial Fund Quarterly, 41:161-182.

Bidwell, Percy Wells. (1917) "Population Growth Southern New England, 1810-1860," Publications of the American Statistical Association, new series no. 120:813:839.

Bieder, Robert E. (1973) "Kinship as a Factor in Migration", Journal of Marriage and the Family, 35, pp. 429-439.

Billington, Ray Allen. (1960) Westward Expansion: A History of the American Frontier. 4th Edition. New York: Macmillan.

Blumin, Stuart M. (1976) The Urban Threshold: Growth and Change in a Nineteenth-Century American Community. Chicago and London: University of Chicago Press.

Bogue, Allan J. (1963) From Prairie to Cornbelt. London and Chicago: University of Chicago Press.

Bowen, William A. (1978) The Willamette Valley Migration and Settlement on the Oregon Frontier. Seattle and London: University of Washington Press.

Bowers, William L. (1960) "Crawford Township, 1850-1870: A Population Study of a Pioneer Community," Iowa Journal of History, 58:1-30.

Boyd's Binghamton Directory, 1859-60. New York: William H. Boyd.

Boyd's Rome Directory; Also, a Business Directory of Oneida County, 1859-60. Rome, New York: Abbott and Redway.

Boyd's Syracuse Directory, A Business Directory of Onondaga County, 1859-60. Syracuse, New York: Thacher and Lawrence.

Brown, Lawrence A., J. Odland, and R. G. Colledge. (1970) "Migration, Functional Distance and the Urban Hierarchy," Economic Geography, 46:472-485.

Brown, Phillip Leslie. (1966) "People on the Move: The Formation of Ohio's Ethnic Composition, 1870-1900", M. A. Thesis in History, The Ohio State University.

Burton, O. Vernon. (1975) "Ungrateful Servants? Edgefield's Black Reconstruction: Part 1 of the Total History of Edgefiled County, South Carolina." Unpublished Ph. D. Thesis in History, Princeton University.

Bushee, Frederick A. (1899) "The Growth of the Population of Boston," Publications of the American Statistical Association, 6:239-274.

Carrothers, Gerald A. (1956) "An Historical Review of the Gravity and Potential Concepts of Human Interaction," Journal of the American Institute of Planners, 22:94-102.

Chudacoff, Howard. (1972) Mobile Americans: Residential

and Social Mobility in Omaha, 1880-1920. New York: Oxford University Press.

Coale, Ansley J.   and Paul Demeny.   (1966) Regional Model Life Tables and Stable Populations. Princeton, New Jersey: Princeton University Press.

Coleman, Peter J.   (1962)   "Restless   Grant   County: Americans on the Move",   Wisconsin   Magazine   of   History, 46:16-20.

Condran, Gretchen A.   and   Eileen   Crimmins.   (1980) "Mortality   differentials between rural and urban areas of states   in   the   northeastern   United   States   1890-1900," Journal of Historical Geograhy, 6:179-202.

Conklin,   Henry.   (1974)   Through   Poverty's   Vale   A Hardscrabble   Boyhood   in   Upstate   New   York,   1832-1862. Syracuse, New York: Syracuse University Press.

Conway, Dennis.   (1980) "Step-Wise Migration: Toward a Clarification of the Mechanism,"   International   Migration Review, 14:3-14.

Conzen, Michael.   (1971) Frontier Farming in an Urban Shadow.   Madison,   Wisconsin: State Historical Society of Wisconsin.

_____.   (1974)   "Local   Migration   Systems   in Nineteenth-Century Iowa," Geographical Review, 64:339-361.

Curti, Merle.   (1959) The Making of an American Community: A Case Study in Democracy in a Frontier County.   Stanford, California: Stanford University Press.

Darroch, A. Gordon.   (1981) "Migrants   in   the   Nineteenth Century: Fugitives   or   Families   in Motion?," Journal of Family History, 6:257-277.

Debow, J. D. B.   (1854)   Statistical   View   of the   United States Washington: Beverley Tucker, Senate Printer.

Deutschman, Harold D.   (1972)   "The   Residential Location Decision: Study of Residential   Mobility,"   Socio-Economic Planning Sciences, 6:349-364.

DeVanzo, Julie.   (1976) Why Families Move: A Model of the Geographical   Mobility   of   Married   Couples. Santa Monica, California: The Rand Corporation, Paper No.   R-1972-DOL.

Doherty, Robert.   (1977)   Society   and   Power   Five   New

England Towns 1800-1860. Amherst, Massachusetts: University of Massachusetts Press.

Doyle, Don Harrison. (1978) The Social Order of a Frontier Community Jacksonville, Illinois 1825-70. Urbana, Chicago, and London: University of Illinois Press.

Dunlevy, James A. and Henry A. Gemeny. (1977) "The Role of Migrant Stock and Lagged Migration in the Settlement Patterns of Nineteenth Century Immigrants," Review of Economics and Statistics, 59:137-144.

Easterlin, Richard A. (1971) "Does Human Fertility Adjust of the Environment?", American Economic Review, 61:399-407.

Ehrlich, Richard L. (1972) "Development of Manufacturing in Selected Counties in the Erie Canal Corridor, 1815-1860." Unpublished Ph. D. Thesis in History, State University of New York at Buffalo.

Ellemers, J. E. (1964) "The Determinants of Emigration: An Analysis of Dutch Studies on Migration," Sociologia Neerlandica, 2:41-55.

Ellis, David Maldwyn. (1946) Landlords and Farmers in the Hudson-Mohawk Region 1790-1850. Ithaca, New York: Cornell University Press.

Engerman, Stanley L. (1975) "Up or Out: Social History and Geographic Mobility in the United States", Journal of Interdisciplinary History, 3:469-489.

Erickson, Charlotte. (1972) Invisible Immigrants: The Adaptation of English and Scottish Immigrants in Nineteenth-Century America. Coral Gables, Florida: University of Miami Press.

Esslinger, Dean R. (1975) Immigrants and the City: Ethnicity and Mobility in a Nineteenth Century Midwestern Community. Port Washington, New York: Kennikat Press.

Fletcher, Henry J. (1895a) "The Doom of the Small Town", The Forum, 19:214-223.

_____. (1895b) "The Drift of Population to Cities: Remedies", The Forum, 19:737-745.

French, John Homer. (1860) Gazetteer of the State of New York. Syracuse: R. P. Smith.

Friedlander, Dov and R. J. Rosheir. (1966) "A Study of Internal Migration in England and Wales: Part I," Population Studies, 19:239-279.

_____. (1966) "A Study of Internal Migration in England and Wales: Part II," Population Studies, 20:45-59.

Gagan, David P. and Herbert Mays. (1973) "Historical Demography and Canadian Social History: Family and Land in Peel County, Ontario," Canadian Historical Review, 14:27-47.

Glasco, Laurence A. (1973) "Ethnicity and Social Structure: Irish, Germans and Native-born of Buffalo, New York, 1850-1860." Unpublished Ph. D. Thesis in History, State University of New York at Buffalo.

_____. (1978) "Migration and Adjustment in the Nineteenth Century City: Occupation Property and Household Structure of Native-born Whites, Buffalo, New York, 1855." In Tamara Harevan and Maris Vinovskis, eds. Family and Population in Nineteenth Century America. Princeton: Princeton University Press.

Goldstein Sidney. (1954) "City Directories as Sources of Migration Data," American Journal of Sociology, 60:169-176.

_____. (1958) Patterns of Mobility, 1910-1950: The Norristown Study. Philadelphia: University of Pennsylvania Press.

Greenwood, Michael J. (1969) "An Analysis of the Determinants of Geographical Labor Mobility in the United States," Review of Economics and Statistics, 51:189-194.

Griffen, Clyde. (1969) "Workers Divided: The Effect of Craft and Ethnic Differences in Pouhgkeepsie, New York: 1850-1880." In Stephen Thernstrom and Richard Sennett, eds., Nineteenth Century Cities: Essays in the New Urban History. New Haven, Connecticut: Yale University Press.

_____ and Sally Griffen. (1978) Natives and Newcomers The Ordering of Opportunity in Mid-Nineteenth-Century Poughkeepsie. Cambridge, Massachusetts and London, England: Harvard University Press.

Hagerstrand, Torsten. (1947) "En landsbygdsbefolknings flyttningsrorelser. Studier over migrationen pa grundval av Asby sockens flyttingslangder 1840-1944," Svensk geografisk arsbok, 23:114-142. Cited in Sivert Langholm.

(1975) "Short-Distance Migration, Circles and Flows: Movement to and from Ullensaker According to the Population Census Lists of 1865," Scandinavian Economic History Review, 23:36-62.

_____. (1962) "Geographical Measurements of Migration." In Jean Sutter, ed., Les Deplacements Humains. Monaco: Hachette.

Hershberg, Theodore, Michael Katz, Stuart Blumin, Laurence Glasco, and Clyde Griffen. (1974) "Occupation and Ethnicity in Five Nineteenth-Century Cities: A Collaborative Inquiry," Historical Methods Newsletter, 7:174-216.

Hodes, Frederick A. (1973) "The Urbanization of St. Louis: a Study in Urban Residential Patterns in the Nineteenth Century." Unpublished Ph. D. Thesis in History, Saint Louis University.

Holbrook, Stewart H. (1950) The Yankee Exodus: An Account of Migration from New England. New York: Macmillan.

Hollingsworth, Thomas H. (1970) Migration Occasional Papers No. 12, University of Glasgow Social and Economic Studies. Edinburgh: Oliver and Boyd.

Hopkins, Richard J. (1968) "Occupational and Geographic Mobility in Atlanta, 1870-1896" Journal of Southern History, 34:200-213.

Hough, Franklin B. (1857) Census of the State of New York for 1855. Albany: Charles Van Benthuysen.

_____. (1867) Census of the State of New York for 1865. Albany: Charles Van Benthuysen and Sons.

Hudson, John C. (1973) "Two Dakota Homestead Frontiers," Annals of the Association of American Geographers, 63:442-462.

_____. (1976) "Migration to an American Frontier," Annals of the Association of the American Geographers, 66:242-265.

Huffman, Frank J., Jr. (1974) "Old South, New South: Continuity and Change in a Georgia County, 1850-1880." Unpublished Ph. D. Thesis in History, Yale University.

Jackson, Susan. (1978) "Movin' on: Mobility through Houston in the 1850s," Southwestern Historical Quarterly, 81:251-282.

Jaffee, A. J. (1940) "Differential Fertility in the White Population in Early America," Journal of Heredity, 31:407-411.

_____ and W. I. Lourie, Jr. (1942) "An Abridged Life Table for the White Population of the United States in 1830," Human Biology, 14:352-371.

Jensen, Richard. (1978) "New Presses for Old Grapes: I: Multiple Classification Analysis," Historical Methods, 11:174-176.

_____, Charles Stephenson, and Jan Reiff Webster. (1978) "Social Predictors of American Mobility: A Census Capture-Recapture Study of New York and Wisconsin, 1875-1905." Unpublished report prepared by the Family and Community History Center of the Newberry Library, Chicago, for the Metro Center, National Institute of Mental Health.

Johnston, R. J. (1971) "Resistence to Migration and the Mover/Stayer Dichotomy: Aspects of Kinship and Population Stability in an English Rural Area", Geografiska Annaler, 53 B:16-27.

Jordan, Terry G. (1966) German Seed in Texas Soil: Immigrant Farmers in Nineteenth-Century Texas. Austin, Texas: University of Texas Press.

Katz, Michael B. (1975) The People of Hamilton, Canada West: Family and Class in a Mid-Nineteenth-Century City. Cambridge, Massachusetts: Harvard University Press.

_____, Michael J. Doucet, and Mark J. Stern. (1978) "Migration and the Social Order in Erie County, New York: 1855," Journal of Interdisciplinary History, 8:669-702.

Kero, Reino. (1977) "The Character and Significance of Migration Traditions from Finland to North America," American Studies in Scandinavia, 9:95-104.

Kirk, Gordon W., Jr. and Carolyn Tyrrin Kirk. (1974) "Migration, Mobility and the Transformation of the Occupational Structure in an Immigrant Community: Holland, Michigan, 1850-80," Journal of Social History, 7:142-164.

Knights, Peter R. (1969) "City Directories as Aids to Ante-Bellum Urban Studies: A Research Note," Historical Methods, 2:1-10.

_____. (1971) The Plain People of Boston, 1830-1860: A Study in City Growth. New York: Oxford University Press.

_____. (1982) Personal Communication. November 18.

Langholm, Sivert. (1975) "Short-Distance Migration, Circles and Flows: Movement to and from Ullensaker According to the Population Census Lists of 1865," Scandinavian Economic History Review, 23:36-62.

Lansing, John B. and Eva Mueller. (1967) The Geographical Mobility of Labor. Ann Arbor: Survey Research Center, University of Michigan.

Laslett, Barbara. (1977) "Social Change and the Family: Los Angeles, 1850-1870," American Sociological Review, 42:268-291.

Lathrop, Barnes F. (1948) "Migration into East Texas 1835-1860," Southwestern Historical Quarterly, 52:1-31, 184-208, 325-348.

Leaman, J. Harold and E. C. Conkling. (1975) "Transport Change and Agricultural Specialization," Annals of the Association of American Geographers, 65:425-432.

Lee, Everett. (1966) "A Theory of Migration," Demography, 3:47-57.

_____. (1970) "Migration in Relation to Education, Intellect, and Social Structure," Population Index, 36:437-444.

Long, Larry H. (1973) "New Estimates of Migration Expectancy in the United States," Journal of the American Statistical Association, 68:37-43.

Lowenthal, David and Lambros Comitas. (1962) "Emigration and Depopulation: Some Neglected Aspects of Population Geography," Geographical Review, 52:195-210.

MacDonald, John S. and Leatrice D. MacDonald. (1964) "Chain Migration, Ethnic Neighborhood Formation, and Social Networks," Milbank Memorial Fund Quarterly, 42:82-97.

Malin, James C. (1935) "The Turnover of Farm Population in Kansas," Kansas Historical Quarterly, 4:339-359.

Mangalam, J. J. (1968) Human Migration A Guide to Migration Literature in English 1955-1962. Lexington: Univerisity of Kentucky Press.

Manring, Randall C. (1978) "Population and Agriculture in

Nodaway, County, Missouri 1850 to 1880," _Missouri Historical Review_, 72:388-411.

Mathews, Lois K. (1909) _The Expansion of New England_. Boston: Houghton Mifflin.

McInnis, Marvin. (1969) "Provincial Migration and Differential Economic Opportunity," in Leroy O. Stone, ed., _Migration in Canada_. Ottawa: Dominion Bureau of Statistics.

Merk, Frederick. (1978) _History of the Westward Movement_. New York: Alfred A. Knopf.

Meyer, Douglas K. (1976) "Native-born Immigrant Clusters on the Illinois Frontier," _Proceedings of the Association of American Geographers_, xx:41-44.

Middleton, J. H. (1905) "Growth of the New York State Census," _Publications of the American Statistical Association_, 9:292-306.

Miles, Henry A. (1845) _Lowell as It Was and as It Is_. Lowell, Massachusetts: Powers and Bagley.

Miller, Ann R. (1965) "Migration Differentials Among Occupation Groups: U. S. 1960," paper presented at the United Nations World Population Conference.

Miller, Robert Gay B. (1973) "City and Hinterland: The Relationship between Urban Growth and Regional Development in Nineteenth Century New York," Unpublished Ph. D. Thesis in History, University of Minnesota.

Modell, John. (1971) "The Peopling of a Working Class Ward: Reading, Pennsylvania, 1850," _Journal of Social History_, 5:71-95.

Morgan, Myfanwy and Hilda H. Golden. (1979) "Immigrant Families in an Industrial City: A Study of Households in Holyoke, 1880," _Journal of Family History_, 4:59-68.

Morrison, Peter A. (1970) "Chronic Movers and the Future Redistribution of Population: A Longitudinal Analysis." Santa Monica, California: The Rand Corporation, P-4440.

Myers, George C., Robert McGinnis, and George Masnick. (1967) "The Duration of Residence Approach to a Dynamic Stochastic Model of Internal Migration: A Test of the Axiom of Cumulative Inertia," _Eugenics Quarterly_, 14:121-126.

Nelson, Phillip. (1959) "Migration, Real Income and Information," Journal of Regional Science, 1:43-74.

New York. Vol. 566. R. G. Dun and Company Collection, Baker Library, Harvard University Graduate School of Business Administration.

New York, Secretary of State. (1855) "Instructions for taking the census of the State of New York in the year 1855." Albany, New York: Weed, Parsons, and Co.

New York State. Census Manuscripts for the 1855 State Census.

New York State. Census Manuscripts for the 1865 State Census.

Nie, Norman H., C. Hadlai Hull, Jean G. Jenkins, Karin Steinbrenner, and Dale H. Bent. (1975) Statistical Package for the Social Sciences. New York: McGraw-Hill.

Nott, Charles C. (1889) "A Good Farm for Nothing", The Nation. November 21:406-408.

Ostergren, Robert C. (1976) "Rattvik to Isanti. A community transplanted," Unpublished Ph. D. Thesis in Geography, University of Minnesota.

_____. (1981) "Land and Family in Rural Immigrant Communities," Annals of the Association of American Geographers, 71:400-411.

Pessen, Edward. (1972) "The Occupations of the Ante-Bellum Rich: A Misleading Clue to the Sources and Extent of their Wealth," Historical Methods Newsletter, 5:49-52.

Population of the United States in 1860 (1864) Washington: Government Printing Office.

(The) Poughkeepsie Directory for 1859-1860. Poughkeepsie, New York: Osborn and Killey.

Price, Daniel O. and Melanie M. Sikes. (1975) Rural-Urban Migration Research in the United States Annotated Bibliography and Synthesis. Bethesda, Maryland: Center for Population Research, U. S. Department of Health, Education, and Welfare.

Ravenstein, E. G. (1876) "Census of the British Isles, 1871: Birthplaces and migration," Geographical Magazine, 3:173-177, 201-206, 229-^33.

_____. (1885) "The laws of migration," _Journal of the Royal Statistical Society_, 48:167-227.

_____. (1889) "The laws of migration," _Journal of the Royal Statistical Society_, 52:214-301.

Records of the Reformed Church in the Village of Gilboa and of the Reformed Church in old Village of Blenheim. Edited by Royden Woodward Vosburgh. Typescript dated February, 1918, at the Schoharie County Historical Society Library, Old Stone Fort Museum, Schoharie, New York.

Records of the Reformed Church in the Town of Schoharie. Edited by Royden Woodward Vosburgh. Typescript dated January, 1918, at the Schoharie County Historical Society Library, Old Stone Fort Museum, Schoharie, New York.

Records of St. Paul's Evangelical Lutheran Church in the Town of Schoharie, Schoharie County, New York. 3 vols. Edited by Royden Woodward Vosburgh. New York: New York Genealogical and Biographical Society, March, 1915.

Redford, Arthur. (1926) _Labour Migration in England, 1800-1850_. Manchester: University of Manchester Press.

Report of the Superintendent of the Census for December 1, 1852. Washington: Robert Armstrong Printer, 1853.

Rice, John G. and Robert C. Ostergren. (1978) "The Decision to Emigrate: A Study in Diffusion," _Geografiska Annaler_, 60B:1-15.

Richmond, Anthony H. (1969) "Sociology of Migration in Industrial and Post-Industrial Societies," in J. A. Jackson, ed., _Migration_. Cambridge: Cambridge University Press.

Ritchey, P. Neal. (1976) Explanations of Migration," in _Annual Review of Sociology_, vol. 2:363-404.

Rose, Arnold M. (1958) "Distance of Migration and Socio-Economic Status of Migrants," _American Sociological Review_, 23:420-423.

Roseman, Curtis C. (1969) "Partial and Total Displacement Migration: A Theoretical and Empirical Examination of Migration in a Total Movement Framework." Unpublished Ph. D. Thesis in Geography, University of Iowa.

_____. (1971a) "Channelization of Migration Flows from the Rural South to the Industrial Midwest," _Proceedings_, Association of American Geographers, 3:140-146.

_____. (1971b) "Migration as a Spatial and Temporal Process," Annals of the Association of American Geographers, 61:589-598.

Sears, Irwin. (1960) "Growth of Population in Philadelphia: 1860 to 1910," Unpublished Ph. D. Thesis in History, New York University.

Schenectady City and County Directory, 1860-61. Schenectady, New York: W. M. Colborne.

Schlesinger, Arthur. (1973) Rise of the City. New York: Macmillan.

(The) Schoharie Patriot. January 1, 1850 through December 31, 1861.

(The) Schoharie Republican. January 1, 1850 through December 31, 1861.

Shannon, Fred A. (1945) "A Post-Mortem on the Labor-Safety-Valve Theory," Agricultural History, 19:31-37.

Shaw, R. Paul. (1975) Migration Theory and Fact. Philadelphia: Regional Science Research Institute, Bibliography Series Number Five.

Spear, Dorothea N. (1961) Bibliography of American Directories Through 1860 Worcester, Massachusetts: American Antiquarian Society.

Speare, Jr., Alden. (1970) "Home Ownership, Life Cycle Stage, and Residential Mobility," Demography, 7:449-458.

Stephenson, Charles. (1980a) "The Methodology of Historical Census Record Linkage: A User's Guide to the SOUNDEX," Journal of Family History, 5:112-115.

_____. (1980b) "Migration and Mobility in Late Nineteenth and Early Twentieth Century America." Unpublished Ph. D. Thesis in History, University of Wisconsin-Madison.

Stillwell, Lewis. (1937) "Migration from Vermont, 1776-1860", Proceedings of the Vermont Historical Society Montpelier, Vermont.

Stouffer, Samuel A. (1940) "Intervening opportunities: a theory relating mobility and distance," American Sociological Review, 5:845-867.

_____. (1960) "Intervening Opportunities and Competing Migrants," Journal of Regional Science, 2:1-26.

Svalestuen, Andres A. (1977) "Five Local Studies of Nordic Emigration and Migration," American Studies in Scandinavia , 9:17-63.

Taeuber, Karl E., W. Haenszel, M. G. Sirkin, and L. Chiazze, Jr. (1968) Migration in the United States: An Analysis of Residential Histories. Health Monograph No. 77, Public Health Service, United States Department of Health, Education, and Welfare.

Tank, Robert M. (1978) "Mobility and Occupational Structure on the Late Nineteenth Century Urban Frontier: The Case of Denver, Colorado," Pacific Historical Review, 47:189-216.

Tarver, James D. (1964) "Occupational Migration Differentials," Social Forces, 43:231-241.

Thernstrom, Stephen. (1964) Poverty and Progress - Social Mobility in a Nineteenth Century City. Cambridge, Massachusetts: Harvard University Press.

_____. (1968) Urbanization, Migration, and Social Mobility in Late Nineteenth-Century America." In Barton J. Bernstein, ed., Towards a New Past Dissenting Essays in American History. New York: Random House.

_____. (1973) The Other Bostonians. Cambridge, Massachusetts: Harvard University Press.

_____ and Peter Knights. (1971) "Men in Motion: Some Data and Speculations about Urban Population Mobility in Nineteenth Century America," In Tamara Harevan, ed., Anonymous Americans: Explorations in Nineteenth-Century Social History. Englewood Cliffs, New Jersey: Prentice-Hall.

Thistlewaite, Frank. (1960) "Migrations from Europe Overseas in the Nineteenth and Twentieth Centuries," XIe Congres International des Sciences Historiques, Rapports, vol. 5. Stockholm.

Thomas, Dorothy Swaine. (1938) Research Memorandum on Migration Differentials. New York: Social Science Research Council Bulletin, No. 43.

Thorne, Mildred. (1959) "A Population Study of an Iowa County in 1850," Iowa Journal of History, 57:305-339.

Tilly, Charles. (1974) _An Urban World_. Boston: Little, Brown.

_____ and C. Harold Brown. (1967) "On Uprooting, Kinship and the Auspices of Migration," _International Journal of Comparative Sociology_, 8:139-164.

(The) _Troy Directory for 1859-1860_. Boston: Adams, Sampson, and Co.

Truesdell, Leon E. (1949) "The Development of the Urban-Rural Classification in the United States: 1874 to 1949." _Current Population Reports_, Series P-23, No. 1. Washington, D. C.: United States Government Printing Office.

Tucker, R. S. (1940) "The Frontier as an Outlet for Surplus Labor," _Southern Economic Journal_, 7:158-186.

Turner, Frederick Jackson. (1920) _The Frontier in American History_. New York: Henry Holt and Co.

_____. (1935) _The United States: The Nation and its Sections_. New York: Henry Holt and Co.

United States. _Manuscripts for the Eighth Census of the United States_.

Unruh, John David. (1979) _The Plains Across: the overland emigrants and the trans-Mississippi West, 1840-60_. Urbana: University of Illinois Press.

(The) _Utica City Directory for 1860-61_. Utica, New York: Joseph Arnott.

Veder, M. A. (1889) _The Nation_, November 28:431.

Vinovskis, Maris A. (1972) "Mortality Rates and Trends in Massachusetts Before 1860," _Journal of Economic History_, 32:184-213.

Wade, Richard C. (1967) _The Urban Frontier: The Rise of Western Cities, 1790-1830_. Cambridge, Massachusetts: Harvard University Press.

Wall, Richard. (1978) "The Age at Leaving Home," _Journal of Family History_, 3:181-202.

Ward, David. (1971) _Cities and Immigrants: A Geography of Change in Nineteenth Century America_. New York, London, and Toronto: Oxford University Press.

Weaver, Herbert. (1945) Mississippi Farmers, 1850-1860. Nashville, Tennessee: Vanderbilt University Press.

Weber, Adna Ferrin. (1899) The Growth of Cities in the Nineteenth Century: A Study in Statistics. New York: Columbia University Press.

_____. (1904) "The Significance of Recent City Growth: The Era of Small Industrial Centres," Annals of the American Academy of Political and Social Science, 23:223-236.

Willcox, Walter F. (1895) "The Decrease of Interstate Migration," Political Science Quarterly, 10:603-614.

Wilson, Harold Fisher. (1936) The Hill Country of Northern New England: Its Social and Economic History, 1790-1930. New York: Columbia University Press.

Wolpert, Julian. (1965) "Behavioral Aspects of the Decision to Migrate," Papers, Regional Science Assocation, 15:159-169.

Worthman, Paul B. (1971) "Working Class Mobility in Birmingham, Alabama, 1880-1914." In Tamara E. Harevan, ed., Anonymous Americans: Explorations in Nineteenth-Century Social History. Englewood Cliffs, New Jersey: Prentice-Hall.

Yans-McLaughlin, Virginia. (1977) Family and Community: Italian Immigrants in Buffalo, 1880-1930. Ithaca, New York: Cornell University Press.

Yasuba, Yasakichi. (1962) Birth Rates of the White Population in the United States, 1800-1860: An Economic Study. Baltimore, Maryland: Johns Hopkins University Press.

Zelinsky, Wilbur. (1962) "Changes in the Geographic Patterns of Rural Population in the United States, 1790-1960", Geographical Review, 52:492-524.

_____. (1973) Cultural Geography of the United States. Englewood Cliffs, New Jersey: Prentice-Hall.

Zipf, Georg K. (1946) "The PlP2/D Hypothesis: On the Inter-City Movement of Persons," American Sociological Review, 11:677-686.

www.ingramcontent.com/pod-product-compliance
Ingram Content Group UK Ltd.
Pitfield, Milton Keynes, MK11 3LW, UK
UKHW020858280225
455677UK00006B/95